THE INNER REVOLUTION

Essays on the Social Sciences in History

harper torchbooks

A reference-list of Harper Torchbooks, classified by subjects, is printed at the end of this volume.

THE INNER REVOLUTION

Essays on the Social Sciences in History

THOMAS C. COCHRAN
UNIVERSITY OF PENNSYLVANIA

HARPER TORCHBOOKS
THE ACADEMY LIBRARY
HARPER & ROW, PUBLISHERS
NEW YORK, EVANSTON AND LONDON

Contents

I: The Inner Revolution

Advanced thinkers of the seventeenth century warned that science had taken God away from nature and from man. Early in the century John Donne lamented that the world was maimed and cursed:

> And new philosophy calls all in doubt,
> The element of fire is quite put out;
> The sun is lost, and the earth
> And freely men confess that this world is spent,[1]

But in spite of the implications read into the new Galilian cosmology religion survived and flourished, and nowhere more than in the northern colonies of America. The Puritans, Quakers and other dissenting sects built religious precepts and language into the growing society, and the middle class character of American life fostered continuing religious strength.

Consequently, the weakening of religious certainties and religious behavior that had come gradually over generations to Europeans occurred rapidly in America from the 1890's on. And weakening religious beliefs had more effect on the rest of the value structure of American middle class society than seems to have been the case elsewhere.

It was in this atmosphere that Americans turned to the study

[1] "An Anatomy of the World," *The Poems of John Donne: From the Text of the Edition of 1633*, 2 vols. (New York. The Grolier Club, 1895), v. II, p. 80.

1

of social science, and a few saw history in a new role. A society sure of its values had needed history only to celebrate the glories of the past, but a society of changing values and consequent confusion also needed history as a utilitarian guide. Hence the social science approach to history, illustrated in this book, arose largely from the inner destruction of values, from the loss of the historic certainties of 19th century Americans. The seminal importance of this inner revolution in values calls for more analysis of some of its details.

I

The basic weapon of destruction in America, as in Europe, was the skeptical, experimental attitude of science. A series of discoveries around the turn-of-the-century in fields as diverse as physics and psychology were more emotionally upsetting than any scientific findings since those of Galileo. In the first quarter of the twentieth century new scientific ideas and attitudes permeated the means, such as child-rearing and schooling, by which the old culture was sustained. While among the middle and upper class groups that could consciously espouse new learning there had been some skepticism in the nineteenth century, in 1900 social behavior based on Christian morality, study of the Bible, and the use of a religious language were still generally the rule. The fact that, historically, a disproportionately large part of the professional elite had been of New England origin had probably helped to spread and preserve religious values in the late nineteenth century. These leaders had made a cold peace with the older science, including evolution, and had continued to preach, and to a degree practice, the virtues associated with a divinely directed society.[2] On the secular front, classic laissez-faire and an equally unscientific Social Darwinism joined with

___

[2] It is not necessary to argue whether or not the American complex of middle class values was primarily religious. The point is that religious values were recognized and accepted.

Christian morality in providing clear, if somewhat contradictory, laws and principles for the conduct of a society.[3]

Before World War I only an advance guard of Americans had absorbed the upsetting scientific ideas, but by 1925 the well educated urban leaders of opinion saw their relations with the world and the universe in new scientific contexts. Aided by social and economic forces an inner revolution had occurred. The cultural change was not the result of any one line of reasoning following from a particular scientific statement. The upsurge of learning and research accompanying the growth of science, resulting technological changes and ultimately new conditions of living all operated to alter attitudes within American culture. As John Dewey saw the process in 1899: "Habits of living are altered with startling abruptness and thoroughness; the search for truths is infinitely stimulated and facilitated and their application to life made not only practicable but commercially necessary. Even our moral and religious ideas and interests . . . are profoundly affected."[4]

In America the cumulative force of belief in the need for experimentation, in the inapplicability of traditional values to a changed present, in the concealed pitfalls of rationality and in the relativity of truth must be seen against a background of heavy non-Protestant immigration, the physical inadequacies of unplanned cities, the rapid growth of bureaucracy, and the great promise of new technology. The essence of the resulting change was not the supercession of an old set of values by new ones, as had occurred in the Protestant Reformation, but rather the demolition of a central part of the value structure with no substitutes offered. The nineteenth century American whether conservative or radical, religious or atheistic recognized the existence of certain fixed values that he had to be for or against. By 1925 the well-educated man was skeptical regarding principles or

[3] See Henry F. May, *The End of American Innocence* (New York: Alfred A. Knopf, 1959), pp. 9-10.
[4] "School and Society" in *Dewey on Education* (New York: Teachers College, 1959), pp. 35-36.

values whether in bringing up his children or forecasting the business situation.

II

Physics and psychology, in particular, forced the intellectual world to consider the profound meanings inherent in their methods and findings, but the thrust of the advanced thinking in these two sciences was reenforced by almost equally significant work in other fields such as biology. While, obviously, no survey of the hypotheses of science upsetting to major social values can be attempted, a brief description of the most significant work in psychology and physics is an essential background for understanding the inner revolution.

Late nineteenth century experimental psychology and other scientific approaches such as historical analysis of the Bible and anthropological study of human behavior cast doubt on the authority of many older moral values. William James' *The Principles of Psychology,* published in 1890, was one of the earliest books to spread the new scientific ideas. "The human being who appears in James' psychology," writes Edna Headereder, "bears little resemblance to the rational man of earlier years."[5] Later in the decade John Dewey, as we shall see, began applying the new psychology to child-rearing and education.

During the next generation academic psychologists were effectively undermining the religious ideas of will power and rationally controlled activity, but for the educated urban middle class the theories of Sigmund Freud were more dramatic and exciting. The popularity of his ideas in the United States in the 1920's fitted the social trends arising from urban industrialism as well as from the whole complex of experimental attitudes. History texts emphasize how the initial Freudian emphasis on sexual repression as a primary cause of neurosis fitted well with post-war ideas regarding elimination of the double standard of morality and more freedom for women. Bringing sex "into the

[5] *Seven Psychologies* (New York: The Century Co., 1933), p. 198.

open" went with short skirts and equality with men in smoking, drinking, language, and voting. But the more important and lasting effect of Freudianism, one that later revisions scarcely weakened, was to cast doubt on the objectivity of reason. Rational processes according to Freud were guided by unconscious urges. Given the same situation two "reasonable" men would, because of different infantile sexual repressions, select facts that reached different conclusions. While later clinical experience has broadened the scope of what is repressed, and lengthened the period over which the unconscious is conditioned, these later scholars have not restored confidence in reason and conscious "will power" as guides to conduct. Ideas have remained ideologies, and truth relative to its context.

In the United States, particularly, the attack on reason was carried to an extreme. Experiments with the conditioned reflex in animals led the University of Chicago psychologist, John B. Watson, to advance a system called Behaviorism in which all "thought" was merely the verbalizing of conditioned reactions.[6] The existence of consciousness was held to be a delusion akin to religion, myths, and other superstitions. While too extreme to convince the majority of experimental psychologists, a few big university departments were won over to Watson's views. Easier to understand than Freud, and more concerned with normal psychology, many middle-class parents became Behaviorists. Behaviorism also influenced writers on child-rearing and was specifically incorporated in *Infant and Child Care,* a booklet widely distributed by the U. S. Department of Labor.[7]

While Watson made all morality a matter of conditioning rather than thought or will, Freud, in effect, turned old-fashioned American morality upside down. Repression of self-indulgence by the use of will power in order to abide by divine precepts was now seen as psychologically dangerous in the case of the

[6] John B. Watson, "Psychology as the Behaviorist Views It," *Psychological Review,* vol. 20 (1913), pp. 158-177. His most influential book was *Psychology from the Standpoint of a Behaviorist* (New York, 1919).

[7] William E. Leuchtenburg, *Perils of Prosperity* (Chicago: University of Chicago Press, 1958), p. 163.

young and probably futile in the case of adults. The repressed desire would find some alternate and perhaps more subtly dangerous form of expression. As in the case of Freudian ideas regarding sex, the new morality, or amorality, of indulgence suited other social trends. A relatively mature industrialism in the 1920's was emphasizing greater consumption. Since from 1923 on lower-class purchasing power per capita was scarcely increasing, greater consumption had to come from luxury spending by the upper income groups—those who were most influenced by the new psychological ideas.

So the older American morality of abstinence, frugality, and saving was for many replaced by an acceptance of promiscuity, high consumption, and living on credit. As with Behaviorism, later attitudes have modified some of the revolutionary extremes of the 1920's, but the general acceptance of the view of mental processes generated by Freud's theories remained the rule in medicine and the social sciences. It is also interesting that the continuing needs of the economy, written into respectable economic doctrine by John Maynard Keynes, prevented a return to earlier views on the immorality of high-level mass consumption.

III

Physics joined psychology in showing the limitations of both verbal logic and sensory perception. The roots of the upsetting knowledge that man could not perceive the nature of the physical world through his senses or describe its processes by verbal logic goes back at least to Clark Maxwell's work on electromagnetism in England in the 1870's. But the philosophical significance of this earlier work was not clear to many intellectuals before Einstein's dramatic solution in 1905 to the paradox of the transit of Mercury. His field equations based on treating space, time, velocity and mass as dependent variables became widely known, if not understood, before World War I. More upsetting in the long run to any mental image of the nature of things was the work done by Lord Rutherford, Max

Planck, and Nils Bohr in the second decade of the century on the structure of the atom and the nature of energy. The net result was to show that ultimate substance, if such existed, was so infinitely small in relation to the space it seemed to occupy as to be negligible, and that what we perceived as matter was an extremely complex structure of electrical relationships. As John Langdon-Davies put it: "Science . . . has taken the very ground from under our feet and substituted a nightmare myriad of atomic and solar systems."[8]

All of this knowledge was deduced from the interpretation of indirect tests and expanded into theories by mathematical logic. When existing mathematics would not provide answers which accorded with the data, as in the case of Planck's quantum theory, new systems of mathematics were developed. To some devout physical scientists, like Sir James Jeans, God could be pictured as the master mathematician.[9]

Although this might seem to go back to the Thomist view of the essential rationality of God, the new rationality was expressed in a flexible mathematical logic incomprehensible to the common man. It was difficult to convey the new theories even to non-mathematical intellectuals. But the fact that physics had destroyed the old concepts of the universe and its matter was widely known by the end of World War I. The hope that physics had opened the door to a new age of faith was not substantiated. The more general reaction appears to have been doubt regarding man's ability to understand the nature of his environment, and increased skepticism regarding all doctrine.

IV

The reaction against traditional forms or values and the rise of radical experimentation that were encouraged directly or indirectly by the new science can be seen in all the arts. But

[8] *The New Age of Faith* (New York: The Viking Press, 1925) , p. 18.
[9] Sir James Jeans, *The Mysterious Universe* (New York: Macmillan, 1932) , pp. 172 ff.

even a brief account of the trends in music, painting, sculpture, architecture, design, poetry, and literature would raise controversies unimportant from the standpoint of our two main theses. Here attention will be focused on philosophy, the social sciences, religion, child-rearing and education; on parts of the culture in which the effects of the new science and its attitudes were direct and largely explicit. These also include the chief agencies by which the culture shapes the personality and learning of successive generations.

Philosophy was directly challenged by the new methods and concepts of physics. A generation of philosophers, led in the second decade by Bertrand Russell in England and Ludwig Wittgenstein in Germany, contended that philosophy should forego its quest for metaphysical conclusions and devote itself to a scientific study of the nature of truth or systems of verification.[10] This narrowing of the scope of philosophical inquiry was resisted by many academic philosophers such as Americans Paul E. More and Irving Babbitt who defended a classical humanism, but most of the younger philosophers followed Russell and Wittgenstein. The result of this refocusing of attention on the nature of logic, rather than on philosophical systems was to make philosophy into a second order discipline unlikely to provide new values or goals, one concerned with means rather than ends.[11] Whereas William James, for example, had advocated a pragmatism in which truth was discovered by experiment, reason, and some divine intuition, his successor, John Dewey, evolved more precise statements of truth in relation to given contexts, statements that apparently left no room for intuition, divine guidance or other metaphysics.[12]

[10] Wittgenstein later moved to England. His book, *The Tractatus*, translated into English in 1922, became the most influential philosophical publication in the 1920's. See also George E. Moore, *Philosophical Studies* (New York: Humanities Press, 1951, orig. ed. 1922).

[11] See Morton White, *Toward Reunion in Philosophy* (Cambridge: Harvard University Press, 1956), pp. 10 ff.

[12] Dewey wrote in 1910: "The abandonment by intelligence of a fixed and static moral end was the necessary precondition of a free and progressive science . . ." *The Influence of Darwin on Philosophy* (New York, 1910), p. 56.

The pause for questioning forced on philosophy by mathematical logic was quickly reflected in the social sciences. The scholars in each discipline became more acutely conscious of the problems of verification and objectivity in their own work. Furthermore, in their research sociologists and economists had somewhat the same type of experiences as the natural scientists. What had seemed to be simple systems controlled by a few variables turned out to be infinitely complex aggregates concerning which theorizing had to be highly tentative. In part this was the usual result of more intensive research, but also involved was the relentlessly questioning attitude arising from knowledge of the problems of natural science. The more philosophically minded historians were forced to recognize the extreme difficulty of verifying any important generalization, recognize the elusive character of true objectivity, and to adopt Dewey's concept of contextual relativism.

These trends in learning illustrate the pervasive character of the change in the highly educated man's view of his situation. But for the change to affect Americans as a whole, the new ideas had to penetrate to the central beliefs of middle-class culture: to attitudes toward religion, child-rearing and education.

V

Because of the strong impact of Spencer's Social Darwinism in the United States, and the rise of critical historiography in the seminaries in the late 1880's, religion felt some of the pressures of the new scientific attitudes more quickly than most phases of American life. Andrew D. White's *A History of the Warfare of Science with Theology in Christendom,* published in 1896, was widely read. The more basic influence of science, however, seems not the attack on certain theological assumptions, which always find new defenses, but the undermining of general religious authority in the more liberal Protestant churches, and as a result forcing appeals for support to rest on social rather than on theological grounds.

European writers such as Ortega y Gasset would urge that man had been "coming out of Christianity" from 1400 on, and historians can argue that this process had been going on in America since 1620.[13] They point out that New England Calvinism quickly departed from European theology in order to hold the support of Americans. But in spite of substituting less rigorous doctrine for irrevocable predestination the churches had preserved their ultimate moral authority.[14] No matter how much some businessmen and politicians disregarded Christian ethics they felt it wise to talk the language of Protestant doctrine, and many, like John D. Rockefeller and J. Pierpont Morgan, were devout believers.

The change from the mid-1890's to the mid-1920's was subtle but basic. As the advanced Protestant churches in the larger cities tried to move in the direction of rendering social service by means of Sunday schools, parish houses, social clubs and missionary work aimed more at social than religious advance, the ministry became more influenced by the ideas of the parishoners. The successful preacher in a prosperous urban parish sought through experiment to achieve a good adjustment, to be a good businessman and a good social leader.

Thus educated urban Protestants (and one might say the same for Jews) had come to apply the questioning attitudes of science to their religious life. Faith survived, but it was in the background. It was not the active implicit faith of the mid-nineteenth century. Parishoners valued their church as a social institution; doctrine was approached more pragmatically on the basis of its credibility and utility; church attendance was seen as a social as well as a religious ritual. The offspring of the immigrants who poured in at the turn of the century tended to sim-

[13] Jose Ortega y Gasset, *Man and Crisis* (New York: W. W. Norton, 1958), p. 198.
[14] See Perry Miller, *The New England Mind from Colony to Province* (Cambridge: Harvard University Press, 1953).

ilar views. "The church to them was only too often just one of
the many ethnic institutions that had to be maintained. . ."[15]

VI

Invading the old-time religious preserves of child-rearing and
education, the experimental psychologists, psychoanalysts, and
educational specialists insured the perpetuation of the new attitudes through altered personality in the ensuing generation.
Since material on child-rearing practices is notably absent from
biographies and autobiographies change must be chiefly inferred
from the written advice offered to parents.[16] Analysis of some
of the available literature from 1865 to 1929 shows the same
tempo of scientific invasion of this sensitive area that is illustrated in other conceptual systems.

In the nineteenth century parents were primarily urged to
teach children to know right from wrong, to be respectful of
authority and to be reverent toward God. In order to be fit
for the life hereafter children were particularly trained to avoid
the many guises of evil. The naughty child should be told: you
have grieved your parents, "but you have grieved your Heavenly
Father much more, you must ask him to forgive you and to
help you to be a better child."[17] There was still the assumed
unity of divine and natural law establishing what was right
and wrong. "Unity in nature and man is the moral, pedagogical
and religious solution of our time," wrote the veteran educator
Emma Marwedel in 1887.[18] "The church, the school, and the

[15] Will Herberg, *Protestant—Catholic—Jew* (New York: Doubleday & Co.,
1955) , p. 31.
[16] I am indebted to Stanley Bailis for this information from his doctoral
dissertation in progress on American Autobiographies.
[17] Mary Allen West, *Childhood: Its Care and Culture* (Chicago: Law, *King
'Law*, 1888), p. 138. Miss West was a specialist who had studied children in
"thousands of homes." For this and the following references I am indebted
to Rosamond B. Cochran for research on late nineteenth and early twentieth century educational and child-rearing writing.
[18] *Conscious Motherhood* (Boston: D. C. Heath, 1887), p. 83. Emma Marwedel brought the ideas of Froebel to bear on American child-rearing and
education from 1871 on.

home all aim at the higher moral culture."[19] The First Com-
mandment to honor thy parents contains according to Mary
Allen West, "an implied command to parents, and furnishes
strong ground for claiming God's authority for the careful training of children."[20] The religious tone in the period before 1890
was no doubt strengthened by the fact that a large part of the
advisors on child rearing were women and ministers, while very
few were doctors.[21]

By the 1890's new psychological ideas were lessening the emphasis on strict, arbitrary discipline and increasing advocacy
of freedom of expression for the child.[22] In the Preface to Felix
Adler's *The Moral Instruction of Children*, W. T. Harris, Com-
missioner of Education, wrote: "the new ideal regards insight
into the reasonableness of moral commands as the chief end."[23]
In this same year Florence H. Winterburn contended that
"Parenthood is already looked upon by the more advanced
minds as a profession, the time will come when its studies will
be reduced to an exact science, ignorance of which will be in-
excusable; as it is even now deplorable."[24] But one suspects that
regardless of what the "more advanced minds" were thinking
most parents still sided with Kate Douglas Wiggin who parodied
the new freedom with the limerick:

> There once was a hopeful young horse
> Who was brought up on love, without force;

[19] *Ibid.*, p. 250.
[20] West, *Childhood*, p. 37.
[21] See for example, Jacob Abbott, *Gentle Measures in the Management
and Training of Children* (New York: Harper & Brothers, 1871); Julia
McNeir Wright, *Practical Life or Ways and Means for Developing Character
and Resources* (Phila: J. C. McCurdy, 1881) Mary E. Sherwood, *Amenities
of Home* (New York: Appleton, 1882); C. E. Sargent, *Our Home or the Key
to a Nobler Life* (Springfield, Mass.: W. C. King, 1884); and Rev. W. F.
Crafts, *Childhood: The Text-Book of the Age for Parents, Pastors and
Teachers* (Boston: Lee and Shepard, 1875).
[22] See Julian Hawthorne, "Make-Believe" in *Childhood*, Vol. I (1892-93),
pp. 18 ff.; Adelaide G. Lytton, "The Washington Pickaninny," *Ibid.*, pp.
23 ff.; Kate J. Wells, "The Futility of a Lie" *Ibid.*, p. 88; and other articles
in this short lived periodical.
[23] New York: Appleton, 1895, p. vi.
[24] *Nursery Ethics* (New York: Baker and Taylor, 1895), p. 151.

He had his own way, and they sugared his hay;
So he never was naughty, of course.[25]

By about 1905 the effects of the new scientific attitudes were beginning to be more apparent. There was more emphasis on introspection by parents, and original sin and depravity were generally rejected. The effect of scientific questioning is reflected in Ernest H. Abbott's note that in religious training our ancestors had an advantage: "They knew very definitely what they wished their children to do and to believe. . . . Now, although they wish to give their children a full complement of doctrines, they either do not possess the full complement themselves, or do not believe that their children are mature enough to receive it."[26] On the whole, however, Geoffrey H. Steere has found that the admonitions were still in terms of divine will and recognized principles.[27] Attitudes toward sex differed little from the "Victorianism" of the nineteenth century.

By the 1920's the revolution had occurred. "The predominately religiously oriented text was an anomaly."[28] The measures advanced were generally in terms of psychology or physiology. Writing in 1920, the Editor of *Mothers Magazine and Home Life* came out squarely for experimentation. The child "cannot learn it by looking at it simply or listening to words that adults use to describe it."[29] He warned the mother that "the more she limits her child, the more she handicaps him in his struggle to learn the world in which he must live."[30] Parents were urged to be friends with their children rather than dis-

[25] Kate Douglas Wiggin wrote articles for *Scribner's, Cosmopolitan,* and *Babyhood* in 1892 that were put in book form in *Children's Rights* (Boston: Houghton Mifflin, 1899). The poem is from p. 146; see also pp. 19 ff., 122, 146 f., 164.
[26] *On the Training of Parents* (Boston: Houghton, Mifflin, 1908), p. 123.
[27] Geoffrey H. Steere, "Changing Values in Child Socialization: A Study of United States Child-Rearing Literature, 1865-1929." Manuscript Thesis, University of Pennsylvania, 1964.
[28] *Ibid.* Ch. IV.
[29] M. V. O'Shea, *First Steps in Child Training* (Chicago: Frederick J. Drake, 1920), p. 25.
[30] *Ibid.,* p. 28.

ciplinarians.[31] In contrast to the clergymen and laymen of the earlier periods, the authors were mainly doctors. While there was an emphasis on permissiveness for the child and self-study for the parent, no principles were stated with the unquestioning confidence of the earlier times. Authoritarian parents of the old religious type could find little support in the textbooks. Freudian attitudes toward sex training were usually present, either explicitly or implicitly. In a word, children were being trained not for the hereafter, but for pragmatic adjustment to a changing present.[32]

The new psychologies that affected the life of the middle class child at home altered the environment of the same child in the next most important institution in shaping personality—the school. The mid-nineteenth century educational philosophy of Horace Mann has been called a "blend of natural law, faith in progress, capitalistic morality, and liberal Protestantism."[33] Late nineteenth century education was still built around the inculcation of Christian moral truths. "The function of the schools," said John Dewey, "was to indoctrinate their students with a positive pattern of beliefs, political and moral axioms and principles that would guide their acts as citizens."[34]

As early as the 1880's American scholars educated in Germany began to bring back both ideas regarding experimental psychology and methods of teaching. Johan Herbart, an early nineteenth century German educator, was one of the precursors of the twentieth century transformation. He urged the teacher to study the child as well as the lesson. He also advocated courses such as history and geography that were useful for good citizenship. In the 1890's the Herbartians exercised a strong influence on the National Education Association, and formed a society of their own.

But the great world leader in undermining the old moralistic,

[31] ibid.
[32] Steere, "Child Socialization." Ch. IV.
[33] Lawrence A. Cremin, *The Transformation of the School* (New York: Alfred A. Knopf, 1961) , p. 10.
[34] Oscar Handlin, *John Dewey's Challenge to Education* (New York: Harper & Brothers, 1959) , p. 24.

authoritarian education was John Dewey. Since he was also an instigator of rebellion in philosophy and the social sciences, Dewey is probably the most ubiquitous American representative of the new experimental attitudes. His whole system of thought in both philosophy and education was based on the methods of experimental science. "A humane society," he thought, "would use scientific method and intelligence with its best equipment to bring about human consequences."[35] He called the elementary school which he organized at the University of ·Chicago in 1896 "The Experimental School." The next year he wrote "it is impossible to tell just what civilization will be twenty years from now. Hence it is impossible to prepare the child for any precise set of conditions."[36] Dewey, "suspicious of all attempts to erect a hierarchy of values," could obviously not supply the basis for a new structure of belief.[37]

While from 1896 on Dewey exerted a strong influence on educational thought, his system spread at first to only a few private schools. Not until 1907 were his ideas incorporated in a major public school system.[38] His great influence on the public schools occurred through the work of disciples after World War I. In 1904 Dewey had come to Columbia where Teacher's College was the major graduate training center for school teachers. A National Society for Progressive Education, formed in 1919, and educational articles and textbooks by his Columbia colleagues, such as William H. Kilpatrick and Harold Rugg, spread the doctrine of child-centered education. While few public schools could afford a completely progressive system, the Dewey principles were known, perhaps in exaggerated form, to every well-educated teacher. Child-centrism reached its peak in the 1920's and then declined, but the strong emphasis on community relations that survived it was scarcely nearer to the old inculcation of fixed moral values.

[35] *Individualism Old and New* (New York: G. P. Putnam's, Capricorn paperback, 1962), p. 138.
[36] "My Pedagogic Creed," *Dewey on Education*, p. 31.
[37] Dewey, *Individualism*, p. 141.
[38] Gary, Indiana; see Lawrence Cremin, *Transformation of the School*, p. 154.

Science also influenced education through quite different channels. The scientific management vogue from about 1910 to the
1920's was reflected in educational administration. In 1911 the
National Education Association appointed a Committee on
Economy of Time in Education which issued four widely read
reports between 1916 and 1919. Their major emphasis was on
elimination of non-essential studies.[39] School boards subjected
teachers' activities to job analysis, and the uses of school funds
were studied on a "scientific" accounting basis. In the resulting
rise of school management the teaching function tended to take
second place. From the management standpoint the function of
the school was to prepare useful, conventional citizens. To a
degree, this was the opposite of the aims of progressive education, but both shared in the attack on older educational values.[40]
Both attacked the traditional content of education, both replaced indoctrination in Christian morality with an emphasis
on community relations. The study of languages declined, political science and history tended to become civics or social
studies with a primary emphasis on adjustment to current social
rather than permanent natural or divine norms. Education had
been revised to turn out citizens with cooperative attitudes and
lightly held beliefs.

This brief review of some of the social effects of the rise of
a pervasive attitude of scientific questioning and skepticism suggests that these early years of the twentieth century may have
been one of the major periods of destruction of traditional
values. However, this proposition may be judged from the Western World in general, there seems little doubt about the magnitude of the change in the United States. The middle and
upper class generations born after 1910 found themselves surrounded by the rubble of once imposing structures of truth.
This alteration of the coordinates in which the individual saw
the mystery of his relations to the world, whether in family life,
education, religion or social values, was a change comparable

[39] *Ibid.* p. 193.
[40] See Raymond E. Calahan, *Education and the Cult of Efficiency* (Chicago: University of Chicago Press, 1962).

to that from the late middle ages to the early modern, but very much more rapid.

The earlier change is widely regarded as having produced a new, dominant type of modal personality variously called Faustian, inner-directed, or capitalistic.[41] The change of the twentieth century is currently held to have brought to dominance a modal type of personality lacking in strong inner convictions and more in need of external approval than the earlier type. Various writers have called this type the marketer, the fixer, the organization man, and the other-directed man.[42] As the names imply the causes selected to account for the twentieth century change stem from the social conditions of mass-production industrialism. David Riesman, for example, attributes the rise of other-direction to incipient decline in population, material abundance, leisure, and bureaucracy—a world in which other people are the problem.[43] William A. Whyte Jr., a non-academic writer whose views have been highly influential, sees his "organization man" as the result of men "belonging" to large bureaucratic enterprises, business, professional or governmental.[44]

While these and other theories based on changes in the economic and demographic environment appear to rest on plausible assumptions, their premises seem inadequate fully to account for the magnitude of the changes in values. Abundance, leisure, and bureaucracy, for example, operate externally and on the adult. It seems equally probable that motive power for the inner revolution was contributed to by the less emphasized spread of the new findings and experimental attitudes of science with the attendant changes in child-rearing, religious training and schooling.

But the question of causal explanation is less important than the generally accepted result. Deeply disturbed by an imper-

[41] David Riesman et al., *The Lonely Crowd* (New Haven: Yale University Press, 1950), pp. 28 ff.; Shepard B. Clough and Charles W. Cole, *Economic History of Europe* (Boston: D. C. Heath, 1946), pp. 81 ff.; R. H. Tawney, *Religion and the Rise of Capitalism* (New York: Penguin Books, 1947), "Preface to 1937 Edition," passim.

[42] Riesman, *The Lonely Crowd*, p. 35.

[43] *Ibid.*, pp. 33-34.

[44] *The Organization Man* (Garden City: Doubleday, Anchor Books, 1957), pp. 3-4.

sonal, rapidly-changing world with relativistic values, men asked new questions of history. In spite of wars and revolutions the last few decades have not been a period for high tragedy or exciting drama, but rather one of continual questioning. History, if it is to hold its high place in the field of learning, must suggest policies for meeting current problems. It is with history in this utilitarian form that the rest of this book is concerned.

II: Historical Use of the
Social Sciences*

The inclusion of history as a full-fledged cooperating member of the social science group has not appealed to most historians in the United States.[1] They see difficulties in the way of such a union that range from philosophic doubt regarding the possibility of a "social" science, to objections to new terminology. Possibly there is feeling of loss in exchanging the free creativity of the artist for the more restricted methods of science. A Macaulay in his study casting a past society in his own mold, and judging it accordingly, was an individual master of the universe he surveyed. While the historian trying to be a social scientist is largely the slave of other people's knowledge and hypotheses, often he may feel that he is a mere feeder-in of data to satisfy theoretical models. Perhaps the younger generation of historians in the United States, even less certain as to their values, are more favorably inclined to this role than their elders, but the evidence is still inconclusive.

United States graduate training in history, stressing neither philosophical attitudes nor social science concepts, has set the inner revolution aside and proceeded on the basis of an undefined "common sense." Resistance to a more intensive study of

---

* Reprinted from *Estralto da Relazioni del X Congresso International di Scienza Storiche*, vol. I, Roma, 1955.
[1] For indifference or objections of historians to defining a propositional or scientific basis for their methods see: *Theory and Practice in Historical Study: A Report of the Committee on Historiography* (Bulletin 54, New York; Social Science Research Council 1946), pp. vii-viii.

either basic values or social science has been based as much on
indifference, on a feeling that common sense is good enough, as
on strongly held opposing views. Many historians incline to see
no necessity for insisting on an explicit orientation.

There is, quite properly, a choice of method dictated by purpose. History written to inspire a popular audience with respect for continuing traditions may rest on the aesthetic appeal
of the presentation, and history, designed consciously or not, to
document a point of view may depend on persuasive rhetoric.
But history used as an effort to find repetitive or probable relationships between past events demands some type of systematic
method.[2]

Unfortunately the social sciences are in their infancy. Aside
from economics and political science the specialized disciplines
are scarcely seventy-five years old. A large part of the basic concepts now being tested in anthropology, sociology, and social
psychology are the creation of the present generation of scholars.
As a consequence all social science knowledge is in flux, and conclusions lack the relative permanence of scientific laws. Robert K.
Merton says of his own discipline:[3]

The growing contributions of sociological theory to its sister-
disciplines lie more in the realm of general sociological orientations
than in that of specific confirmed hypotheses. . . . Despite the many
volumes dealing with the history of sociological theory and despite
the plethora of empirical investigations, sociologists (including the
writer) may discuss the logical criteria of sociological laws without
citing a single instance which fully satisfied these criteria.

The question, therefore, is not a philosophical one of what
some ideal, mature social sciences could contribute to historical

---

[2] In this connection, it should be noted that writers such as R. G. Colling-
wood claim that historical understanding is of a unique and immediate
character. History is held to be made up of human thoughts and experience, and the historian is able to relive these experiences in his imagination. A brief statement and refutation of this theory may be seen in W. H.
Walsh, *Philosophy of History* (New York: Harper Torchbooks, 1961), pp.
48-71.

[3] R. K. Merton, *Social Theory and Social Structure: Toward the Codifica-
tion of Theory and Research* (Glencoe, Ill.: Free Press, 1949) , pp. 86, 92.

understanding, but an immediate practical one of what can to-day's social science contribute? It is this pragmatic aspect that leads me to stress personal experience in proposing answers to the question. A few specific instances illustrating how social science knowledge or methods have proved useful in various types of situations seem more likely to carry weight than a host of abstract generalizations.[4]

Before turning to such examples, however, it should be noted that experience has indicated some general difficulties in the way of a merger between history and the social sciences. The relationship of advance conceptualization to historical source materials is one of the chief areas of misunderstanding. Purely deductive theory has value in stimulating the historian's imagination, but is seldom directly applicable to his material. The type of concepts or hypotheses being argued for here are those that have arisen from other empirical data. To this extent the argument does not deny that the materials come first. But the materials to be examined should not be confined to the specific letters or reports that constitute the "sources". Just as a broad knowledge of the secondary historical writing on his problem enables the historian to take advantage of the investigations of others, a knowledge of what social scientists have thought allows him to take advantage of their inductions from the study of comparable situations. These ideas will direct the historian's attention to aspects of his material that he might otherwise miss, and allow him in turn to suggest changes in the social science concepts.

There are also practical problems in bringing the disciplines together. Many of the areas of research suggested by the social sciences demand close collaboration between the historian and some specialists that is often difficult to arrange. Social scientists are inclined to regard historians as primarily gatherers of facts, as scholars without lively theoretical interests, and are skeptical regarding the applicability of historical materials to present

[4] For a more extended attempt, see *The Social Sciences in Historical Study: A Report of the Committee on Historiography*, Bulletin 64 (New York: Social Science Research Council, 1954).

problems. Historians, on the other hand, are likely to see many social scientists as too specialized and disinterested in broad syntheses. When one adds these mutual doubts to the difficulties always inherent in group activity and to university and professional disciplinary barriers, it is not surprising that relatively little interdisciplinary research is undertaken.

It is not always necessary, however, to undertake the hazards of interdisciplinary research. The historian may learn the social sciences for himself and apply them in his own work. Some conferences with colleagues in the particular social science field involved are desirable, to avoid the kind of misinterpretations that may arise from the printed page, but the historian must in any case re-adapt existing techniques to his kind of material.

I

The first examples of the value of the social sciences to the historian are selected to illustrate the use of advance conceptual plans. Before beginning the history of the Pabst Brewing Company we asked Professor Arthur H. Cole of Harvard University to draw up a list of questions that an economist would ask of business records.[5] The questions suggested a number of problems not generally dealt with by historians. From having attention called to such matters in a formal theoretical way, some of the most interesting aspects of the history emerged. For example questions regarding locational factors and marketing brought out the following relationships:

While the Milwaukee location was excellent, the specific location of the brewery within the city of Milwaukee deteriorated in value. This was due, ironically enough, to the success of the Pabst company

---

[5] A. H. Cole, "Business History and Economy History," *The Journal of Economic History,* Supplement V (December 1945), pp. 51-53; Thomas C. Cochran, *The Pabst Brewing Company, The History of a Business* (New York: New York University Press, 1948). "We" is used not as an affectation, but because in all the research noted in this paper I have been assisted by other scholars.

in helping to change the character of the Milwaukee brewing business. Presumably to ensure dry storage cellars, the plant was built on a low hill instead of on the banks of a nearby navigable river. As long as business was local the extra haul up and down the hill was relatively unimportant, but when the company started shipping beer by boat and railroad, a location inaccessible to either of these forms of transportation was a distinct disadvantage. Furthermore, artificial refrigeration eliminated by 1880 the need for deep storage cellars. Pursuing this factor down to the present day, however, we see that the bad specific location in Milwaukee has led to the development of Pabst plants in other cities, and this may ultimately be a great advantage to the company.

The most compelling locational advantage of Milwaukee over Chicago, Cincinnati, and St. Louis was, ironically again, the smallness of the population which restricted the company's home market. With all other factors favorable to large production and the growth of a shipping business, the Milwaukee brewers were forced into a contest for the national market in order to sell their surplus product at a time when their future rivals in the larger western cities were still content to sell at home.[6]

The historical reader may object at this point that the above illustration represents merely the application of informed common sense to the data. To this objection there can be no sweeping rebuttal. The difference between the application of a well structured group of related concepts, and the intuitive use of common sense is often subtle. The gain resulting from the more systematic procedures may appear mainly in the orderly presentation of the evidence and the explicitness of the conclusions. But granting the staggering problems of the historian, even this gain would seem sufficient to justify the method. Researchers unequipped with the concepts of location theory might have seen clearly the paradox of the Pabst brewery location, but then again they might not.

The same procedure of collecting categories of interest to scholars in other disciplines was pursued in the study of the

[6] Thomas C. Cochran, "The Economics in a Business History," *The Journal of Economic History,* Supplement V (December 1945) , p. 60.

ideas and attitudes of railroad leaders from 1845 to 1890.[7] For this purpose economists, sociologists, political scientists, and social psychologists were consulted. Since the material to be studied was business office correspondence, and research assistance was used, it was doubly important to have explicit reminders of what to look for. Apparent gains from the use of this method in the study will be discussed in more detail in Chapter VII.

The research for both the above books was done by professional historians using conventional sources. A social science approach, however, may suggest the use of materials not generally used by historians. Chief among these are: additional statistical aids such as birth, death, school and tax records, manuscript census reports, and city directories; business, hospital and other institutional records; questionnaires given to carefully chosen samples, and controlled interviews of many different types. In the use of these latter materials it is obvious the historian must decide in advance what he is after. Adjustments may be made as research progresses, but these, in general, will involve repeating the earlier part of the work.

The following illustration of the value of additional types of material in broadening the scope of history involves interdisciplinary team research by representatives of all the social sciences. The history of technological change and social adjustment in Norristown, Pennsylvania from 1900 to 1950 was undertaken at the University of Pennsylvania by a continuing graduate seminar under directors from anthropology, history and sociology.[8] As ultimately interpreted by the staff, technological change and social adjustment included all the subjects that historians could normally expect to explore from the available material. Our interest here is in the additional aspects of the data that traditionally oriented historians might have overlooked.

[7] Thomas C. Cochran, *Railroad Leaders 1845 to 1890: The Business Mind in Action* (Cambridge, Mass., Harvard University Press, 1953), pp. 5-7. Also, *Infra.*, Chapter VII.

[8] At one time or another, Professors Edward P. Hutchinson, Dorothy S. Thomas, Anthony F. C. Wallace, and the author acted as faculty directors of the seminar.

Let us take the matter of population. The historians were not unaware of the importance of population change in any area study, but they would no doubt have been content with use of Federal censuses. The sociologists, however, being trained demographers went much further. To begin with they included in- and out-migration among the prescribed topics for research. Sidney Goldstein, then a graduate student in sociology, later Field Director of the Project, undertook the study of migration. Working with Professor Dorothy S. Thomas, he introduced the group to the problems involved in selecting true random samples, and the use of business directories, school records, and vital statistics as aids to historical population research.

The business directories, issued every two years and purporting to list all inhabitants over eighteen years old were checked against the decennial censuses and found to be substantially accurate.[9] Then random samples of five per cent of the males resident in Norristown were drawn from directories ten years apart for the period 1910 to 1950. From each sample Dr. Goldstein found who had entered the Borough during the previous decade, and who left during the ensuing one. The factor that differentiated this study from any carried out previously for other communities was that by use of school records and vital statistics he could tell with a high degree of accuracy where the members of the sample originated, whether by growing up in Norristown or by in-migration, and for those who disappeared during the following decade, whether they migrated or died.

When Dr. Goldstein examined the results of his research he made an interesting discovery. Of those people in the samples who had been resident in Norristown ten or more years only about 25 per cent left the borough during the following decade, whereas of those who had entered the city during the previous decade more than 50 per cent left during the following one. The city, that is, had two populations living side by side. Fairly

[9] For a more detailed description see Sidney Goldstein, *Patterns of Mobility 1910-1950: The Norristown Study* (Philadelphia: University of Pennsylvania Press, 1958).

permanent residents, many of whom had been born there, and a migrating group that continually came and went.

Judged from crude statistics of population turnover for other cities the Norristown situation was apparently representative. This suggests that United States culture has been divided not only into regional sub-cultures such as northeast or southwest, or rural or urban, but also into migratory and non-migratory categories. If this is the case, the non-migratory group should have been the perpetuators of the regional sub-culture, and the migratory group the spreaders of a standardized national culture. The idea further suggests that there may be ascertainable differences in personality types between the two groups.

From this apparently physical statistical research, therefore, there emerged an important cultural problem that historians using their conventional methods and materials would presumably have overlooked, one that may have important implications for the study of industrial societies, and might also be applied to cultural permanence and change in the American westward movement.

II

Another value of the social sciences for historical study comes from their emphasis on norms, types and averages that will permit the erection of what many scholars call models and what historians would probably refer to as connected propositions or generalizations. Related propositions depending upon orders of magnitude inevitably lead to efforts to measure and quantify historical data.

Economists and sociologists turning to historical study appear to have differed most from historically trained scholars in their greater interest in quantification. Statistical theory offers many helpful techniques. One of the recurrent problems of historical evidence is the mathematical significance of small numbers of cases. If only four Congressmen out of eighty-four for which information could be secured at a certain date had fathers who were farmers, how reliable is this as a guide to the occupation of the fathers of Congressmen in general at this period? Substitution in a simple formula known as the Chi Square Test will provide a mathematical answer.

Yet the other social scientists have not communicated much of this enthusiasm for measurement to American historians. So slight has been the interest of the latter in finding and using norms and averages, even when they are available from government statistics, that some of the most obvious needs have not been met. Educational statistics are usually treated in the most haphazard manner, if at all. Misconceptions regarding industrial growth are perpetuated through failure to examine relevant production series.[10] Crude data regarding national productivity, income and so forth at different dates are frequently used without adjustment for price and population changes. There are no definitions of classes of urban communities at varying dates. The effect of election issues has been discussed by leading historians without proper statistical analysis of the actual votes.

But many social norms or types are not matters to be handled statistically. The desired category may be seen in the evidence as a tendency, a probability, or as possibly representative of a broader group. A type may also be deduced as a research tool in order to emphasize variations from this "ideal" norm in the real data.[11] Historians tend to use this method, but frequently in an inexact uncritical fashion. Westerner, southerner, businessman, the frontier and other ideal types are employed without the kind of definition that would make them into tools for separating the abnormal from the usual.

[10] See Chapter III.
[11] A. Spiethoff, "Pure Theory and Economic Gestalt Theory Ideal Types and Real Types," in F. C. Lane and J. C. Riemersma, eds., *Enterprise and Social Change* (London: George Allen and Unwin, 1953), pp. 451 ff.

III

The social sciences tend to emphasize the uniform characteristics of social processes rather than the unique elements of each situation. This calls attention to the importance of long-run mass phenomena or trends rather than individual events. But both approaches get at aspects of reality, and shifting from one to the other may have a valuable corrective effect.

For example, the historian records the hardships, economic, social and political caused by the long depression of the 1870's in the United States. Even the business cycle theorist using selected series will see the decade as one of less than average prosperity. But if the focus is shifted from these business events to the economy as a whole a radically different picture is presented. The westward movement of people and railroads in the early part of the decade brought great new farming areas into production. As a consequence the supposedly depressed decade of the seventies shows a high rate of increase in per capita gross national product or real national income.[12]

A more striking contrast between basic economic development and the apparent trend of immediate events occurs in relation to the Civil War. American historians have been inclined to regard the Civil War as a great stimulating force in industrialization; in fact, some disregard industrial activity in prewar decades and by inference make the war periodize the coming of the industrial revolution. As explained in Chapter III, the available statistics do not support this conclusion.

The historian turning to quantification or typification of past phenomena often finds that the particular trends whose amplitudes he would record were not measured by contemporaries, and cannot be directly recovered from existing statistics. The relative economic welfare of various groups in society, the efficiency of marketing arrangements or transportation are representative of present interests that cannot be followed by direct

[12] *Historical Statistics of the United States: Colonial Times to 1957* (Washington, 1960), p. 139.

statistics much back of the twentieth century. To estimate these and other unrecorded relationships in earlier society, resort must be had to indices. From this standpoint an index is a datum that implies the co-existence of some other datum. If a relationship may be inferred between the known data and the unrecorded movement under investigation, the index is, at least, suggestive.

Historians have always made use of such evidence, but social scientists have probably given the matter more thought and have developed both ingenious indices, and rigorous tests for meaningful correlations between series.

Earl J. Hamilton, an economist by training, has demonstrated the use of price data as an index of many other social phenomena. Price and wage series, he writes,

disclose changes in the economic positions of different groups such as farmers, fishermen, and industrialists over short periods of time. In combination with data concerning technological development, market relationships, and organizational improvements, price and wage statistics can roughly measure variations in the economic welfare of various groups of producers over periods as long as one or two decades. . . . Changes in the ratio of the prices of staple commodities in widely separated producing and consuming centers over long periods of time register alterations in the efficiency of transportation and distributive systems. Variations in the spread between the prices of finished goods at successive steps in the process of distribution likewise measure the efficiency of mercantile agencies. . . . Perhaps in very few cases has there been a combination of competition imperfect enough and demand elastic enough over periods to prevent prices from reflecting, much better than can other attainable historical data, changes in relative technological efficiency. Only through comparative prices could one possibly know, for example, that, as Beveridge pointed out, the increased efficiency in producing steel in Great Britain since the Black Death has been approximately fifty times as great as in producing wheat. It was his encyclopedic knowledge of American price history that enabled Arthur H. Cole to suggest that increasing command of southern staples, especially cotton, over non-southern commodities after the early 1840's may well have had a bearing on the optimism and political ascendancy of the South in the decade of the 1850's.[13]

These are only a few of the uses that Professor Hamilton finds for price indices.

IV

Social science methods are not limited to quantitative materials. Instead of inferring a relationship between a known statistical series and an unknown movement, the mere appearance of a certain factor may be taken as an indication of the existence of a close or invariable correlative. Here again, historians have often used this method, but social science offers suggestions for greater precision. For example, an organized marketing system may usually have been taken as a correlative of the existence of cities, but it required a new development in economic theory to suggest that product differentiation was a correlative of monopolistic or limited competition. Similarly population growth was presumed for centuries to be inversely correlated to urbanism,[14] but only recently have demographers also pointed to correlation between fertility and the business cycle.

Theoretical constructs or models have value in giving meaning and organization to otherwise diffuse data. The theoretical model does not necessarily have to be true to be useful. In manipulating the empirical findings the model may be modified or destroyed, but almost inevitably the process will have called attention to previously unnoticed characteristics of the evidence. An illustration of this in the study of opinion may be found in Chapter V.

[13] E. J. Hamilton, "Use and Misuse of Price History," *The Journal of Economic History*, Supplement IV (December 1944), pp. 55, 56. For detailed discussion of the use of prices for a limited period of United States history see: A. Bezanson, assisted by B. Daley, M. C. Denison, and M. Hussey, *Prices and Inflation During the American Revolution: Pennsylvania 1700-1790* (Industrial Research Department, Wharton School, University of Pennsylvania, University of Pennsylvania Press, 1951).

[14] See A. O. Aldridge, "Franklin as Demographer," in *The Journal of Economic History*, IX (May 1949), pp. 25-44.

V

Historians are inclined by their training to think in terms of records, to have an almost irresistible urge to delve into a newly opened collection of important papers without regard to what general social problems they will illuminate. Social scientists, on the other hand, tend like the physical scientist to think first in terms of a challenging problem without immediate regard for the materials that may provide an answer. To put it another way, the logic of the developing system of knowledge in each social science discipline raises certain questions. The scholar wants primarily to answer these questions, and he turns to whatever materials seem likely to be useful. As an economist, Alexander Gerschenkron, has expressed it: "Historical research consists essentially in application to empirical material of various sets of empirically derived hypothetical generalizations and in testing the closeness of the resulting fit, in the hope that in this way certain uniformities, certain typical situations, and certain typical relationships among individual factors in these situations can be ascertained".[15]

The differing approaches of historians and social scientists were well illustrated at the Research Center in Entrepreneurial History at Harvard, organized by Arthur H. Cole with the aid of the late Joseph A. Schumpeter and others. The initial research group represented economics, history, sociology, and the interdisciplinary group known at Harvard as Social Relations. The field of study, defined over-simply, was the business man in society as a factor in economic change.[16]

In the beginning the sociologists, particularly Leland H. Jenks, raised the most provocative theoretical questions. But the growth of this theoretical framework proceeded independently of any formal collection of evidence.

Meanwhile the historians following their usual procedures,

[15] A. Gerschenkron, "Economic Backwardness in Historical Perspective," in B. F. Hoselitz, ed., *The Progress of Underdeveloped Areas* (Chicago: University of Chicago Press, 1952), pp. 3-4.
[16] Efforts at achieving tight definition of purpose or precisely uniform views were deliberately avoided by the Center.

were studying business source materials without waiting to formulate exact hypotheses in advance. The Research Center led to easy informal communication between the social scientists and the historians. The latter brought questions arising from studying their materials to the attention of the men from other disciplines, and, in turn, the historians searched their records for data that would support or modify the hypothetical propositions of the sociologists and economists. It was in this context that David Landes and John E. Sawyer applied sociological concepts to qualitative study of the French entrepreneur in the nineteenth century,[17] and role theory was applied to the material on railroad leaders.

In the interplay of trained capacities, or incapacities, the historians were undoubtedly interested by those hypotheses that might be tested by the materials with which they were familiar and somewhat repelled by constructs that seemed difficult to document. But in any case their approach was altered by contact with social scientists in so far as they started with questions and then looked for material that might supply answers.

Hypotheses based on pre-suppositions can be dangerous tools. But so can the implicit or surreptitious pre-suppositions from which no one is free. Of the two dangers, that of implicit bias is by far the greater. Psychologists contend that starting with a well worked out model or series of interrelated questions is perhaps the only reliable aid to objectivity. Since many American historians take the opposite point of view, that a carefully structured theory introduces bias in handling the evidence, and that a relatively blank and "open" mind is best for objective observation, it will be well to illustrate the rather uniformly held views of social psychologists on this matter.

Musafer Sherif has conducted many experiments that show the inability of the individual to avoid surreptitious suggestion

[17] D. S. Landes, "French Entrepreneurship and Industrial Growth in the Nineteenth Century," in *The Journal of Economic History*, IX (May 1949), pp. 45-61; J. E. Sawyer, "The Entrepreneur and the Social Order: France and the United States," in W. Miller, ed., *Men in Business* (Cambridge, Mass.: Harvard University Press, 1952, and also New York: Harper Torchbooks, 1962), pp. 7-22.

or "affect" if he has no system to combat it. One of these experiments graphically illustrates this fact. A tiny point of light shines in a dark room. To most observers the light appears to move. "At first, the movements seem chaotic. But they are remarkably responsive to the experimenter's suggestions; his instructions may cause the light to move rapidly to the right, slowly upward, etc. . . . The fact that external structure is wanting allows maximum play for inner structure-giving factors and for all those which arise in the subject from the verbal and other suggestions of those present."[18] If, however, a thin line of light is placed near the spot, if external structure is supplied, no one can be deluded into seeing motion.

Translating the laboratory experiment into terms of written evidence, the more precise the statement of what is being looked for the less disagreement there will be between scholars as to whether or not that element occurs in a given body of material. Careful advance statement of categories to be examined, questions to be answered, and methods to be used will call attention not only to the anticipated aspects of the evidence but also to those that were not expected. Whereas, if the historian has no external framework for reference these discrepancies might pass unnoticed.

For example, in categories for analysis of the material for Railroad Leaders there was a heading "ideas regarding democratic procedure."[19] In this box it was hoped to put opinions on the participation of junior executives or other employees in policy making. The box remained empty. Had it not been there, however, it would have been difficult for either of those who did the research to be sure that some such opinion had not escaped them because they were not looking for it.

Professor Paul F. Lazarsfeld and Allen Barton, sociologists who have studied the use of categories and questions to give order and weight to apparently qualitative material write: "There is a direct line of logical continuity from qualitative

[18] Gardner Murphy, *Personality: A Bio-social Approach to Origins and Structure* (New York: Harper & Brothers, 1947), pp. 347-348.
[19] Thomas C. Cochran, *Railroad Leaders*, p. 6.

classification to the most rigorous forms of measurement, by way of intermediate devices of systematic ratings, ranking scales, multi-dimensional classifications, typologies, and simple quantitative indices. In this wider sense of measurement, social phenomena are being measured every day. . . ."[20] They urge careful exploration of the logical implications of simple forms of measurement.

One such simple form is "content analysis": noting the frequency of occurrence of certain phrases, concepts, ideas or verbal symbols in a given body of writing. The assumption is that frequency of occurrence will correlate with the interest of the writer or speaker in communicating the idea, and will guard the researcher against being misled by rhetorical emphasis, or his own presuppositions. An application of this technique to historical material can be seen in Ithiel de Sola Pool, *The Prestige Papers*.[21] Editorials in leading newspapers of England, France, Germany, Russia and the United States were studied for the occurrence of some 416 symbols referring to political ideologies from 1890 to the late 1940's. The historian may think that the conclusions did not add greatly to what common sense would lead one to suspect. On this point Bernard Berelson in an introduction that discusses the problems of content analysis, maintains that such studies "develop quantitative measures for concepts previously used on a less formalistic basis. In this monograph the development of an index of stereotyping and instability in political terminology is a case in point. And in the process of verification they qualify the large assumptions that may previously have been made about the nature of political vocabularies over several countries and many years."[22]

---

[20] D. Lerner and H. D. Lasswell, *The Policy Sciences: Recent Developments in Scope and Method* (Stanford: Stanford University Press, 1951), p. 155.

[21] Ithiel de Sola Pool, et al., *The Prestige Papers* (Hoover Institute Studies, Series C: Symbols, No. 2., Stanford University Press, 1951).

[22] *Ibid.*, VI.

VI

So far attention has been focused on aspects of the social sciences and their procedures that have utility for the historian. Lest these present too optimistic a picture, some of the difficulties in using the social sciences should be mentioned.

The problem of the value for history of non-empirical deductive theory has harassed historians for several generations. Sir John Clapham, one of the fathers of economic history in the English speaking world, wrote: "The central problems of economic theory, although they may be stated in terms of a particular historical phase, are in essence independent of history."[23] After listening to sociologist Franklin H. Giddings read a paper on social causation in 1903, George L. Burr, editor of *The American Historical Review,* said: "I have listened with much interest to the speculations of Professor Giddings. They are very fine. They may well be true. But the thing of which Professor Giddings is talking is not history. . . ."[24]

Pure theory is a matter of choosing definitions, and its development has to be in the form of corollaries implicit in those definitions. There is no place in it for empirical, or historical, evidence. The applicability of the initial assumptions to a given situation may be questioned, but once they are accepted the theory follows by inescapable logic.

There is, however, a valid interrelationship between history and pure theory. New elements or lines of investigation that would not occur to the empiricist, whether historian or other social scientist, are often suggested by the results of logical theorizing. Conversely theorists need to know the history of situations in order to make applicable basic assumptions. The two methods should reinforce each other in adding to the scope of awareness.

Another methodological tool of the social sciences that pre-

[23] J. Clapham, "Economic History as a Discipline," in Lane and Riemersma, *Enterprise and Social Change,* p. 419.
[24] *Publications of the American Economic Association,* 3rd series, vol. V (1904), p. 434.

sents difficulties for the historian is the personal interview. As empirical research has gained prestige in anthropology, sociology and social psychology, the personal interview and questionnaire have been increasingly used. Even as applied to current opinion or information, construction of the questionnaire, its administration, and interpretation of the results have to be considered very carefully.[25] Historical information gained by these techniques varies from moderately accurate to practically worthless.

Experience with an administered questionnaire in the Norristown project illustrated the nature of the variation. On factual historical data intimately associated with the interviewee such as former positions and places of residence, answers appeared to be reasonably accurate as to sequence, but weak on exact dates. On less factual personal history such as how leisure time was spent or how the automobile affected their life in former decades the respondents were weak, and in many cases a stereotype was repeated for each time period, although other evidence in the interview contradicted the lack of change. Recollections regarding the character of surrounding society such as changes in neighborhoods or religious attitudes appeared in the average questionnaire to be practically worthless. In these latter categories the answer presumably represented present attitudes projected back in time.[26]

The historical aspects of this part of the Norristown material, however, suffer from the questionnaire having been given to a random sample of the population. This meant that most of the answers came from working class people not used to generalizing regarding their experience. Interviews with citizens selected for their knowledge often yielded richer results, and a score or more of such interviews on the same topics in the same location usually gave internal evidence of whether the statements were true or false. But the results of any single interview, no matter how well informed the person, must be regarded as weak historical evidence.

[25] See H. Hyman, "Interviewing as a Scientific Process," in *The Policy Sciences*, pp. 203-218.
[26] Sidney Goldstein, *The Norristown Study* (Philadelphia: University of Pennsylvania Press, 1961), pp. 60-79.

VII

This chapter has been informal, and illustrative of reading or research that has left a lasting impression upon the author. Obviously no effort has been made systematically to survey the social sciences for those concepts or methods that may be of most use to the historian. Such eclectic procedure seems justifiable. Experience suggests that a social science approach to history is largely one of attitude or spirit. It is characterized by an interest in measurement, norms, precise statement, and systematic conceptual structures.

But an emphasis on system and structure need not prevent the historian from indulging in the imaginative flights that have always been associated with his best achievements. No hypothesis or question need be ruled out as too bizarre or fanciful as long as it is constantly treated as an unproven assumption. In fact, a major weakness of traditional history, one that may be strengthened by social science knowledge, is failure to speculate regarding historically unconventional aspects of the data or situation.

Furthermore, no one should be enslaved by existing social science methods. These are in general short-run rather than long, hence they have failed to take sufficient account of change over time. The historian with his different orientation may and should be an innovator in method, materials, and hypotheses. He should approach social science in the same spirit that led mathematical physicist P. W. Bridgman to write: "I am not one of those who hold that there is a scientific method as such. The scientific method, as far as it is method, is nothing more than doing one's damndest with one's mind, no holds barred."[27]

History as one of the social science disciplines is still history with its intuitive insights and methodological limitations. From inadequate data historians must still piece together qualitative aspects of situations by the process that anthropologist Robert Redfield has called "descriptive integration". Behind the indi-

[27] P. W. Bridgman, "The Prospect for Intelligence," in *Yale Review*, 34 (March 1945), p. 450, quoted in *Bulletin, 64*, Social Science Research Council, p. 30.

vidual exploits of leaders and their rationalization in letters, historians have to try to detect underlying environmental trends from fragmentary statistics and to assume patterns of personality from clues that the social psychologist would consider inadequate. To ask that historians regard parts of their discipline as primarily analytic and synthetic rather than merely descriptive is a call to add to the scope of historical research, to cast off the implied limitations of Professor Burr's statement that the study of social causation as such is "not history", to go beyond the admonition that the historian's main object should be describing events as they actually happened, to seek a broader intellectual approach that includes an interest in social theory; and to recognize that since history is a selection of factors from an infinite universe, an explicit basis for selection reduces misinterpretation.

III: Did the Civil War
Retard Industrialization? *

The preceding chapter has given illustrations of the value of various social science methods. In this chapter a large historical question will be analyzed in some detail by the quantitative, statistical approach common to economists, with results that show how exciting events may obscure or wholly distort what is really happening.

In most textbook and interpretative histories of the United States the Civil War has been assigned a major role in bringing about the industrial revolution in America.[1] Colorful business developments in the North—adoption of new machines, the quick spread of war contracting, the boost given to profits by inflation, the creation of a group of war millionaires— make the war years seem not only a period of rapid economic change but also one that created important forces for future growth. The superficial qualitative evidence is so persuasive that apparently few writers have examined the available long-run statistical series before adding their endorsement to the conventional interpretation. The following quotations taken from the books of two generations of leading scholars illustrate the popular view.[2]

* Reprinted with permission from the *Mississippi Valley Historical Review*, XLVIII, September 1961.
[1] This article is based on a paper presented by the author at the annual meeting of the Mississippi Valley Historical Association in Louisville in April, 1960.
[2] These particular authors are cited merely as examples of historical opinion, not because they are more in error than others. The reader needs only to take down other texts from his own shelf to find similar statements.

"The so-called Civil War," wrote Charles A. and Mary R. Beard in 1927, ". . . was a social war . . . making vast changes in the arrangement of classes, in the accumulation and distribution of wealth, in the course of industrial development."[3] Midway between 1927 and the present, Arthur M. Schlesinger, Sr., wrote: "On these tender industrial growths the Civil War had the effect of a hothouse. For reasons already clear . . . nearly every branch of industry grew lustily."[4] Harold U. Faulkner, whose textbook sales have ranked near or at the top, said in 1954: "In the economic history of the United States the Civil War was extremely important. . . . In the North it speeded the Industrial Revolution and the development of capitalism by the prosperity which it brought to industry."[5] The leading new text of 1957, by Richard Hofstadter, William Miller, and Daniel Aaron, showed no weakening of this interpretation: "The growing demand for farm machinery as well as for the 'sinews of war' led to American industrial expansion. . . . Of necessity, iron, coal, and copper production boomed during the war years."[6] A sophisticated but still essentially misleading view is presented by Gilbert C. Fite and Jim E. Reese in a text of 1959: "The Civil War proved to be a boon to Northern economic development. . . . Industry, for example, was not created by the war, but wartime demands greatly stimulated and encouraged industrial development which already had a good start."[7] In a reappraisal of the Civil War, in *Harper's Magazine* for April 1960, Denis W. Brogan, a specialist in American institutions, wrote: "It may have been only a catalyst but the war precipitated the entry of the United States into the modern

[3] *The Rise of American Civilization* (2 vols., New York, 1927) , vol. II, p. 53.
[4] Homer C. Hockett and Arthur M. Schlesinger, *Land of the Free: A Short History of the American People* (New York, 1944) , p. 355. Schlesinger wrote the section beginning with the Civil War.
[5] *American Economic History* (7th ed., New York: Harper & Brothers, 1954) , p. 345. The same statement appears in a later edition (1960).
[6] *The United States: The History of a Republic* (Englewood Cliffs, New Jersey: Prentice Hall, 1957) , p. 381.
[7] *An Economic History of the United States* (Boston, 1959), p. 284.

industrial world, made 'the take-off' (to use Professor W. W. Rostow's brilliant metaphor) come sooner."[8]

In all of these reiterations of the effect of the Civil War on industrialism statistical series seem to have been largely neglected. None of the authors cited reinforce their interpretations by setting the war period in the context of important long-run indexes of industrial growth. Since 1949, series for the period 1840 to 1890 that would cast doubt on the conventional generalizations have been available in *Historical Statistics of the United States, 1789-1945*.[9] In 1960 a new edition of *Historical Statistics* and the report of the Conference on Research in Income and Wealth on *Trends in the American Economy in the Nineteenth Century* have provided additional material to support the argument that the Civil War retarded American industrial development.[10] These volumes give data for many growth curves for the two decades before and after the war decade—in other words, the long-run trends before and after the event in question. The pattern of these trends is a mixed one which shows no uniform type of change during the Civil War decade, but on balance for the more important series the trend is toward retardation in rates of growth rather than toward acceleration. This fact is evident in many series which economists would regard as basic to economic growth, but in order to keep the discussion within reasonable limits only a few can be considered here.

Robert E. Gallman has compiled new and more accurate series for both "total commodity output," including agriculture, and "value added by manufacture," the two most general measures of economic growth available for this period. He writes: "Between 1839 and 1899 total commodity output in-

[8] "A Fresh Appraisal of the Civil War," *Harper's Magazine* (New York), CCXX (April 1960), p. 140.

[9] U.S. Bureau of the Census, *Historical Statistics of the United States: 1789-1945* (Washington, 1949).

[10] U.S. Bureau of the Census, *Historical Statistics of the United States: Colonial Times to 1957* (Washington, 1960); *Trends in the American Economy in the Nineteenth Century* (Princeton, 1960), published by the National Bureau of Economic Research as Volume XXIV of its *Studies in Income and Wealth*.

creased elevenfold, or at an average decade rate of slightly less than 50 per cent. . . . Actual rates varied fairly widely, high rates appearing during the decades ending with 1854 and 1884, and a very low rate during the decade ending with 1869."[11] From the over-all standpoint this statement indicates the immediately retarding effect of the Civil War on American economic growth, but since most of the misleading statements are made in regard to industrial growth, or particular elements in industrial growth, it is necessary to look in more detail at "value added by manufacture" and some special series. Gallman's series for value added by manufacture in constant dollars of the purchasing power of 1879 shows a rise of 157 per cent from 1839 to 1849; 76 per cent from 1849 to 1859; and only 25 per cent from 1859 to 1869.[12] By the 1870's the more favorable prewar rates were resumed, with an increase of 82 per cent for 1869-1879, and 112 per cent for 1879-1889. Thus two decades of very rapid advance, the 1840's and the 1880's, are separated by thirty years of slower growth which falls to the lowest level in the decade that embraces the Civil War.

Pig-iron production in tons, perhaps the most significant commodity index of nineteenth-century American industrial growth, is available year-by-year from 1854 on. Taking total production for five-year periods, output increased 9 per cent between the block of years from 1856 to 1860 and the block from 1861 to 1865. That even the slight increase might not have been registered except for the fact that 1857 to 1860 were years

[11] *Trends in the American Economy*, p. 15.

[12] *Historical Statistics* (1960 ed.), p. 402. "Constant" or "real" means dollars adjusted to eliminate price changes. It should be remembered that all series expressed in current dollars need to be corrected for rather violent price movements during these fifty years. Precise adjustments would vary with every series, and would involve many problems, but the movement of wholesale prices in general (Warren-Pearson Index) may be roughly summarized as follows. In 1850 prices were 12 per cent lower than in 1840, but by 1860 they were 11 per cent higher than in 1850. From 1860 to 1865 prices rose 99 per cent, but by 1870 the increase for the decade was only 46 per cent. By 1880 the decline for the decade was 26 per cent, and for the decade ending in 1890 it was 18 per cent. *Ibid.*, p. 115. In other words, current dollars are a very unreliable indicator, particularly as applied to wholesale prices.

of intermittent depression is indicated by an 81 per cent increase over the war years in the block of years from 1866 to 1870.[13] If annual production is taken at five-year intervals, starting in 1850, the increase is 24 per cent from 1850 to 1855; 17 per cent from 1855 to 1860; 1 per cent from 1860 to 1865; and 100 per cent from 1865 to 1870. While there is no figure available for 1845, the period from 1840 to 1850 shows 97 per cent increase in shipments, while for the period 1870 to 1880 the increase was 130 per cent. To sum up, depression and war appear to have retarded a curve of production that was tending to rise at a high rate.

Bituminous coal production may be regarded as the next most essential commodity series. After a gain of 199 per cent from 1840 to 1850 this series shows a rather steady pattern of increase at rates varying from 119 to 148 per cent each decade from 1850 to 1890. The war does not appear to have markedly affected the rate of growth.[14]

In the mid-nineteenth century copper production was not a basic series for recording American growth, but since three distinguished authors have singled it out as one of the indexes of the effect of the war on industry it is best to cite the statistics. Before 1845 production of domestic copper was negligible. By 1850 the "annual recoverable content" of copper from United States mines was 728 tons, by 1860 it was 8,064 tons, by 1865 it was 9,520 tons, and by 1870 it was 14,112 tons. In this series of very small quantities, therefore, the increase from 1850 to 1860 was just over 1,000 per cent, from 1860 to 1865 it was 18 per cent, and from 1865 to 1870 it was 48 per cent.[15]

Railroad track, particularly in the United States, was an essential for industrialization. Here both the depression and the war retarded the rate of growth. From 1851 through 1855 a total of 11,627 miles of new track was laid, from 1856 through 1860, only 8,721 miles, and from 1861 through 1865, only 4,076 miles. After the war the rate of growth of the early 1850's was

[13] *Ibid.*, pp. 365-366.
[14] *Ibid.*, p. 357.
[15] *Ibid.*, p. 368.

resumed, with 16,174 miles constructed from 1866 through 1870. Looked at by decades, a rate of over 200 per cent increase per decade in the twenty years before the war was slowed to 70 per cent for the period from 1860 to 1870, with only a 15 per cent increase during the war years. In the next two decades the rate averaged about 75 per cent.[16]

Next to food, cotton textiles may be taken as the most representative consumer-goods industry in the nineteenth century. Interference with the flow of southern cotton had a depressing effect. The number of bales of cotton consumed in United States manufacturing rose 143 per cent from 1840 to 1850 and 47 per cent from 1850 to 1860, but fell by 6 per cent from 1860 to 1870. From then on consumption increased at a little higher rate than in the 1850's.[17]

While woolen textile production is not an important series in the over-all picture of industrial growth, it should be noted that, helped by protection and military needs, consumption of wool for manufacturing more than doubled during the war, and then fell somewhat from 1865 to 1870. But Arthur H. Cole, the historian of the woolen industry, characterizes the years from 1830 to 1870 as a period of growth "not so striking as in the decades before or afterwards."[18]

Immigration to a nation essentially short of labor was unquestionably a stimulant to economic growth. Another country had paid for the immigrant's unproductive youthful years, and he came to the United States ready to contribute his labor at a low cost. The pattern of the curve for annual immigration shows the retarding effect of both depression and war. In the first five years of the 1850's an average of 349,685 immigrants a year came to the United States. From 1856 through 1860 the annual average fell to 169,958, and for the war years of 1861 to 1865 it fell further to 160,345. In the first five postwar years the average rose to 302,620, but not until the first half of the 1870's

[16] *Ibid.*, p. 427-28.
[17] *Historical Statistics* (1949 ed.), p. 187. This table is not carried back to 1840 in the 1960 edition.
[18] Arthur H. Cole, *The American Wool Manufacture* (2 vols., Cambridge: Harvard University Press, 1926), vol. I, p. 392.

did the rate equal that of the early 1850's. Had there been a
return to prosperity instead of war in 1861, it seems reasonable
to suppose that several hundred thousand additional immigrants
would have arrived before 1865.[19]

In the case of farm mechanization the same type of error
occurs as in the annual series on copper production. "Random"
statistics such as the manufacture of 90,000 reapers in 1864 are
frequently cited without putting them in the proper perspective
of the total number in use and the continuing trends. Reaper
and mower sales started upward in the early 1850's and were
large from 1856 on, in spite of the depression. William T.
Hutchinson estimates that most of the 125,000 reapers and
mowers in use in 1861 had been sold during the previous five
years.[20] While the business, without regard to the accidental
coming of the war, was obviously in a stage of very rapid
growth, the war years presented many difficulties and may actually have retarded the rate of increase.[21] Total sales of reapers
for the period 1861-1865 are estimated at 250,000—a quite ordinary increase for a young industry—but the 90,000 figure for
1864, if it is correct, reinforces the evidence from the McCormick
correspondence that this was the one particularly good year of
the period. During these years William S. McCormick was often
of the opinion that the "uncertainties of the times" made advis-
able a suspension of manufacturing until the close of the war.[22]

For a broader view of agricultural mechanization the series
"value of farm implements and machinery" has special interest.
Here the census gives a picture which, if correct, is explicable
only on the basis of wartime destruction. Based on constant
dollars the average value of machinery per farm fell nearly 25
per cent in the decade of the war and showed nearly a 90 per
cent gain in the 1870's.[23] Differing from these census figures is a

[19] *Historical Statistics* (1960 ed.), p. 57.
[20] William T. Hutchinson, *Cyrus Hall McCormick* (2 vols., New York,
1930-1935), vol. II, p. 67.
[21] *Ibid.*, vol. II, pp. 67-95.
[22] *Ibid.*, vol. II, p. 88.
[23] *Historical Statistics* (1960 ed.), p. 285. For price index see note 12,
above.

series prepared by Marvin W. Towne and Wayne D. Rasmussen based on the production of farm machinery. While this obviously does not take account of destruction of existing equipment or the rapid increase in the number of farms, the record of new production is hard to reconcile with the census figures. The production of implements and machinery reckoned in constant dollars is a sharply rising curve from 1850 on, with increases of 110 per cent from 1850 to 1860; 140 per cent from 1860 to 1870; and 95 per cent from 1870 to 1880.[24] Meanwhile the number of farms increased by about one third in each of the decades of the 1850's and 1860's and by one half in the 1870's.[25] Whatever interpretation is given to these figures, it does not appear that the war greatly increased the trend of agricultural mechanization. The series for gross farm product in constant dollars shows wide variations in increase from decade to decade, with the 1860's in the low group. The gains were 23 per cent, 1840 to 1850; 42 per cent, 1850 to 1860; 21 per cent, 1860 to 1870; 52 per cent, 1870 to 1880; and 20 per cent, 1880 to 1890.[26]

Much American business expansion was financed by short-term bank loans continuously renewed. Thus major increases in business activity should be mirrored in increases in bank loans, both for financing short-term transactions and for additions to plant and working capital that would, in fact, be paid off gradually. If there was a really great Civil War boom in business activity it should be indicated in the series "total loans" of all banks. But it is not. In constant dollars, bank loans fell slightly between 1840 and 1850, and rose nearly 50 per cent by 1860. It should be noted that none of these three decadal years were periods of high prosperity. During the war Confederate banking statistics were not reported by the comptroller of the currency, but by 1866 there is a comparable figure for the nation

[24] *Trends in the American Economy,* p. 276.
[25] The percentage increases were 41 per cent (1860 over 1850); 30 per cent (1870 over 1860) ; and 51 per cent (1880 over 1870). *Historical Statistics* (1960 ed.) , p. 278.
[26] *Ibid.,* p. 284.

as a whole, and in constant dollars it is some 35 per cent below that of 1860. Even by 1870 the constant dollar value of all loans was more than 15 per cent lower than just before the war. If instead of examining loans one looks at total assets of all banks the decline in constant dollars from 1860 to 1870 is reduced to 10 per cent, the difference arising from a larger cash position and more investment in government bonds.[27]

Net capital formation would be a more proper index of economic growth than bank loans or assets. Unfortunately, neither the teams of the National Bureau of Economic Research nor those of the Census Bureau have been able to carry any reliable series back of 1869. From colonial times to 1960, however, the chief single form of American capital formation has undoubtedly been building construction. Farm houses, city homes, public buildings, stores, warehouses, and factories have year-by-year constituted, in monetary value, the leading type of capital growth. Gallman has drawn up series for such construction based on estimating the flow of construction materials and adding what appear to be appropriate mark-ups.[28] Admittedly the process is inexact, but because of the importance of construction in reflecting general trends in capital formation it is interesting to see the results. The rate of change for the ten-year period ending in 1854 is about 140 per cent; for the one ending in 1859 it is 90 per cent; for 1869 it is 40 per cent; and for 1879 it is 46 per cent. Taking a long view, from 1839 to 1859 the average decennial rate of increase was about 70 per cent, and from 1869 to 1899 it was about 40 per cent.[29] The rate of advance in construction was declining and the war decade added a further dip to the decline.

Since the decline in rate is for the decade, the exact effect of the war years can only be estimated, but the logic of the situation, reinforced by the record of sharp cut-backs in railroad

[27] *Ibid.*, p. 624. The reader is again warned that deflation of current dollar values for this early period is an inexact process.

[28] *Trends in the American Economy*, pp. 60-64.

[29] *Ibid.*, p. 24. Gallman has two alternate series which I have averaged. For the purposes of this paper either series leads to the same conclusions.

building, seems inescapable: the Civil War, like all modern wars, checked civilian construction. The first year of war was a period of depression and tight credit in the Middle West, which checked residential and farm construction in the area that grew most rapidly before and after the war. In both the East and the West the last two years of the war were a period of rapid inflation which was regarded by businessmen as a temporary wartime phenomenon. The logical result would be to postpone construction for long-term use until after the anticipated deflation. The decline in private railroad construction to a small fraction of the normal rate exemplifies the situation.

Lavish expenditure and speculation by a small group of war contractors and market operators gambling on the inflation seem to have created a legend of high prosperity during the war years. But the general series on fluctuations in the volume of business do not bear this out. Leonard P. Ayres's estimates of business activity place the average for 1861 through 1865 below normal, and Norman J. Silberling's business index is below its normal line for all years of the war.[30] Silberling also has an intermediate trend line for business, which smooths out annual fluctuations. This line falls steadily from 1860 to 1869.[31] Much of Silberling's discussion in his chapter "Business Activity, Prices, and Wars" is in answer to his question: "Why does it seem to be true that despite a temporary stimulating effect of war upon some industries, wars are generally associated with a long-term retarding of business growth. . .?"[32] He puts the Civil War in this category.

Collectively these statistical estimates support a conclusion that the Civil War retarded American industrial growth. Presentation of this view has been the chief purpose of this article. To try to judge the non-measurable or indirect effects of the war is extremely difficult. But since further discussion of the conventional qualitative factors may help to explain the prevailing

[30] Leonard P. Ayres, *Turning Points in Business Cycles* (New York, 1939), p. 14; Norman J. Silberling, *The Dynamics of Business* (New York, 1943), p. 50.
[31] Silberling, *The Dynamics of Business*, p. 61.
[32] *Ibid.*, p. 66.

evaluation in American textbooks, it seems appropriate to add some conjectural *obiter dicta.*

Experience with the apparently stimulating effects of twentieth-century wars on production makes the conclusion that victorious war may retard the growth of an industrial state seem paradoxical, and no doubt accounts in part for the use of detached bits of quantitative data to emphasize the Civil War's industrial importance.[33] The resolution of the paradox may be found in contemporary conditions in the United States and in the nature of the wartime demand. The essential wastefulness of war from the standpoint of economic growth was obscured by the accident that both of the great European wars of the twentieth century began when the United States had a high level of unemployment. The immediate effect of each, therefore, was to put men to work, to increase the national product, and to create an aura of prosperity. Presumably, the United States of the mid-nineteenth century tended to operate close enough to full employment in average years that any wasteful labor-consuming activities were a burden rather than a stimulant.

By modern standards the Civil War was still unmechanized. It was fought with rifles, bayonets, and sabers by men on foot or horseback. Artillery was more used than in previous wars, but was still a relatively minor consumer of iron and steel. The railroad was also brought into use, but the building of military lines offset only a small percentage of the over-all drop from the prewar level of civilian railroad construction. Had all of these things not been true, the Confederacy with its small industrial development could never have fought over four years of increasingly effective blockade.

In spite of the failure of direct quantitative evidence to show accelerating effects of the war on rates of economic growth, there could be long-run effects of a qualitative type that would gradually foster a more rapid rate of economic growth. The

[33] Ayres, Silberling, and some other students of economic activity such as Herbert Hoover, however, blame the breakdown of the 1930's on the dislocations caused by World War I. *Ibid.,* pp. 65-66. See also *The Memoirs of Herbert Hoover: The Great Depression, 1929-1941* (New York, 1952), p. 105.

most obvious place to look for such indirect effects would be in the results of freeing the slaves. Marxists contended that elimination of slavery was a necessary precursor of the bourgeois industrialism which would lead to the socialist revolution. The creation of a free Negro labor force was, of course, of great long-run importance. In the twentieth century it has led to readjustment of Negro population between the deep South and the northern industrial areas, and to changes in the use of southern land.

But economically the effects of war and emancipation over the period 1840 to 1880 were negative. Richard A. Easterlin writes: "In every southern state, the 1880 level of per capita income originating in commodity production and distribution was below, or at best only slightly above that of 1840. . . . [This] attests strikingly to the impact of that war and the subsequent disruption on the southern economy."[34] In general, the Negroes became sharecroppers or wage laborers, often cultivating the same land and the same crops as before the war. In qualification of the argument that free Negro labor led to more rapid industrialization it should be noted that the South did not keep up with national pace in the growth of non-agricultural wealth until after 1900.[35]

Two indirect effects of the war aided industrial growth to degrees that cannot accurately be measured. These were, first, a more satisfactory money market, and secondly, more security for entrepreneurial activity than in the prewar period. The sharp wartime inflation had the usual effect of transferring income from wage, salary, and interest receivers to those making profits. This meant concentration of savings in the hands of entrepreneurs who would invest in new activities; and this no doubt helps to explain the speculative booms of the last half of the 1860's and first two years of the 1870's which have been treated as the prosperity resulting from the war. Inflation also eased the burdens of those railroads which had excessive mort-

[34] *Trends in the American Economy*, p. 85.
[35] Simon Kuznets, ed., *Population Redistribution and Economic Growth: United States, 1870-1950* (2 vols., Philadelphia, 1957-1960), vol. I (Methodological Considerations and Reference Tables), pp. 729-32; vol. II (Analysis of Economic Change) , p. 109.

gage debts. But a great deal of new research would be needed to establish causal connections between the inflationary reallocation of wealth, 1863 to 1865, and the high rate of industrial progress in the late 1870's and the 1880's.

The National Banking Act, providing a more reliable currency for interstate operations, has been hailed as a great aid to business expansion although it would be hard to demonstrate, aside from a few weeks during panics, that plentiful but occasionally unsound currency had seriously interfered with earlier industrial growth.[36] The existence of two and a half billion dollars in federal bonds also provided a basis for credit that was larger than before the war. This led to broader and more active security markets as well as to easier personal borrowing. But two qualifications must be kept in mind. First, local bank lending to favored borrowers had probably tended to be too liberal before the war and was now put on a somewhat firmer basis. In other words, since 1800 a multiplication of banks had made credit relatively easy to obtain in the United States, and in the North this continued to be the situation. Second, the southern banking system was largely destroyed by the war and had to be rebuilt in the subsequent decades. It should also be remembered that by 1875 some 40 per cent of the banks were outside the national banking system.[37]

Because of a few colorful speculators like Jay Gould, Daniel Drew, and Jim Fisk, and the immortality conferred on them, initially by the literary ability of the Adams brothers, the New York stock exchange in the postwar decade appears to have mirrored a new era of predatory wealth. But one has only to study the scandals of the London and New York stock exchanges in 1854 to see that there was little growth in the sophistication or boldness of stock operators during these fifteen years.[38] In any case, the exploits of market operators were sel-

[36] See Bray Hammond, *Banks and Politics in America: From the Revolution to the Civil War* (Princeton, 1957), pp. 663-67, 670.

[37] *Historical Statistics* (1960 ed.), pp. 628-638.

[38] See James K. Medbury, *Men and Mysteries of Wall Street* (Boston, 1870), pp. 319 ff.; Margaret G. Myers, *The New York Money Market* (2 vols., New York, 1931), vol. I, p. 140.

dom related in a positive way to economic growth. Even a record of new issues of securities, which is lacking for this period would chiefly reflect the flow of capital into railroads, banks, and public utilities rather than into manufacturing. Very few "industrial" shares were publicly marketed before the decade of the 1880's; such enterprises grew chiefly from the reinvestment of earnings.

There was strong government encouragement to entrepreneurial activity during the Civil War, but to ascribe to it unusual importance for economic growth requires both analysis of the results and comparison with other periods. Government in the United States has almost always encouraged entrepreneurs. The federal and state administrations preceding the Civil War could certainly be regarded as friendly to business. They subsidized railroads by land grants, subscribed to corporate bond issues, and remitted taxes on new enterprise.[39] Tariffs were low, but railroad men and many bankers were happy with the situation. Whether or not American industrialism was significantly accelerated by the high protection that commenced with the war is a question that economists will probably never settle.

The building of a subsidized transcontinental railroad, held back by sectional controversies in the 1850's, was authorized along a northern route with the help of federal loans and land grants when the southerners excluded themselves from Congress. Putting more than a hundred million dollars into this project in the latter half of the 1860's, however, may have had an adverse effect on industrial growth. In general, the far western roads were built for speculative and strategic purposes uneconomically ahead of demand. They may for a decade, or even two, have consumed more capital than their transportation services were then worth to the economy.

To sum up this part of the obiter dictum, those who write of

---

[39] Myers, *New York Money Market,* vol. I, p. 296; National Bureau of Economic Research, *Capital Formation and Economic Growth* (Princeton, 1955), p. 382. See also Carter Goodrich, *Government Promotion of American Canals and Railroads, 1800-1890* (New York, 1960).

the war creating a national market tied together by railroads under-estimate both the achievements of the two decades before the war and the ongoing trends of the economy. The nation's business in 1855 was nearly as intersectional as in 1870. Regional animosities did not interfere with trade, nor did these feelings diminish after the war. By the late 1850's the United States was a rapidly maturing industrial state with its major cities connected by rail, its major industries selling in a national market, and blessed or cursed with financiers, security flotations, stock markets, and all the other appurtenances of industrial capitalism.

But when all specific factors of change attributable to the war have been deflated, there is still the possibility that northern victory had enhanced the capitalist spirit, that as a consequence the atmosphere of government in Washington among members of both parties was more friendly to industrial enterprise and to nothern-based national business operations than had formerly been the rule. It can be argued that, in spite of Greenbackers and discontented farmers, legislation presumably favorable to industry could be more readily enacted. The Fourteenth Amendment, for example, had as a by-product greater security for interstate business against state regulation, although it was to be almost two decades before the Supreme Court would give force to this protection. By 1876, a year of deep depression, the two major parties were trying to outdo each other in promises of stimulating economic growth. This highly generalized type of argument is difficult to evaluate, but in qualification of any theory of a sharp change in attitude we should remember that industrialism was growing rapidly from general causes and that by the 1870's it was to be expected that major-party politics would be conforming to this change in American life.

Massive changes in physical environment such as those accompanying the rise of trade at the close of the Middle Ages or the gradual growth of industrialism from the seventeenth century on do not lend themselves readily to exact or brief periodization. If factory industry and mechanized transportation be taken as the chief indexes of early industrialism, its spread in the

United States was continuous and rapid during the entire nineteenth century, but in general, advance was greater during periods of prosperity than in depressions. The first long period without a major depression, after railroads, canals, and steamboats had opened a national market, was from 1843 to 1857. Many economic historians interested in quantitative calculations would regard these years as marking the appearance of an integrated industrial society. Walt W. Rostow, incidentally, starts his "take-off" period in the 1840's and calls it completed by 1860.[40] Others might prefer to avoid any narrow span of years. Few, however, would see a major stimulation to economic growth in the events of the Civil War.

Finally, one may speculate as to why this exaggerated conception of the role of the Civil War in industrialization gained so firm a place in American historiography. The idea fits, of course, into the Marxian frame of revolutionary changes, but it seems initially to have gained acceptance quite independently of Marxian influences. More concentrated study of the war years than of any other four-year span in the nineteenth century called attention to technological and business events usually overlooked. Isolated facts were seized upon without comparing them with similar data for other decades. The desire of teachers for neat periodization was probably a strong factor in quickly placing the interpretation in textbooks; thus, up to 1860 the nation was agricultural, after 1865 it was industrial. Recent study of American cultural themes suggests still another reason. From most standpoints the Civil War was a national disaster, but Americans like to see their history in terms of optimism and progress. Perhaps the war was put in a perspective suited to the culture by seeing it as good because in addition to achieving freedom for the Negro it brought about industrial progress.

[40] W. W. Rostow, *The Stages of Economic Growth* (Cambridge, Eng.: The University Press, 1960), p. 95.

IV: Entrepreneurial History *

The confusions regarding the economic effects of the Civil War emphasize how far we are from seeing American history as an interconnected structure of social relationships. Many important social areas have seldom or never been examined by historians. Between the older business history, which concentrated attention upon the administration of the firm, and general social or economic history, which frequently omitted business processes altogether, there is a broad, vacant area. In this twilight zone lie the relations of business leaders with similar men in other firms, the interactions of businessmen with society as a whole, and the economic and social effects of business decisions. Some scholars saw such a host of related problems in this area that they decided to give it a special name: entrepreneurial history.[1] In defining this field, the term entrepreneur was not restricted to the conventional American textbook meaning of one who risks capital in an enterprise. Rather, the definition put forward by French economist Jean-Baptiste Say in 1814 was re-expressed in broader language to see entrepreneurship as a function often shared by many men in a single firm. In the research of the group, entrepreneurship or business leadership was conceived as operating in a broad socio-economic setting.

* Reprinted with permission from: *The Pennsylvania Magazine of History and Biography*, July 1950.
[1] A Research Center for Entrepreneurial History at Harvard was organized by Arthur H. Cole in 1948.

The systematic pursuit of a new interest of this kind required a series of assumptions as to what should be examined, some tentative hypotheses about relationships and dynamics, and then historical facts against which to test and expand the original concepts. The major assumption of entrepreneurial history is that it requires the exploration of the economic and social roles played by the entrepreneur: how he did his job, and what doing his particular job meant from the standpoint of his personality, his interests, and his other social roles. To gain adequate perspective, these explorations should take place in various historical settings.[2]

What is such study likely to mean for history or the social sciences? for one thing, it should be a corrective for the elimination of man from economic theorizing. The necessity for including the human factor in economic calculations is very obvious when we take a look at the history of a country like Venezuela. Venezuela has all of the factors usually assumed to be necessary for rapid industrial development. It has oil and iron ore, both readily available to water transportation; it has been populated for many years by people who have known of European technology; and one finds it hard in studying its history to discover any conventional economic reason for the failure of these people to develop their resources. Yet Venezuela remained a backward farming country until American oil companies began to develop it following the concessions granted in 1921, and its iron resources remained unexploited until the United States Steel Company entered the picture at a somewhat later date. The answer obviously is that the general culture of Venezuela was not such as to encourage entrepreneurship; or to carry this a step further, economic growth does not depend simply upon a population and a given body of resources and transportation facilities; it depends upon the whole cultural complex that may or may not lead to enterprise, savings, reinvestment of capital, and further development.

The economists, of course, have recognized the importance of

[2] For more on social role see Chapter VII. It is worth noting that although written data may vary in age from a day to five hundred years, any that can be collected are necessarily historical.

entrepreneurship abstractly, but they have not found satisfactory ways to use this factor in setting up their models or developing their theories. More inclusion of entrepreneurship in economic history, for example, will unquestionably reorient it in the direction of anthropoligical and sociological knowledge. It will not necessarily make the businessman a hero, but it will affirm the necessity of seeing economic growth in cultural terms.

For the general historian, it will mean a re-evaluation of the roles and importance of business leaders, particularly in countries such as the United States. Our present history generally has seen business leaders as parasites on a deterministic process. Historians who are in no other way determinists nevertheless seem to assume that our economic development would have gone along in good and productive paths if left to itself, whereas grasping and unscrupulous business leaders deflected this natural progress into antisocial lines for their own advantage. The corrective needed is not a eulogy of business, but more understanding of the social processes which have channeled the economic life of the nation.

An analysis from the period in which many American historians have discussed the businessman, the age of the "robber barons," will illustrate the reinterpretation that may come from entrepreneurial history. The "robber barons" are usually selected from among the railroad, industrial, and financial leaders of the period from about 1865 to 1900, and more often than not are the only businessmen who appear in college textbooks covering this period. According to the present historical mythology, they are seen as "bad" or unusually grasping and unscrupulous types in our culture against the background of a "good" public. The interest in discussing them is to illustrate business malpractices, and, presumably, to convey moralistic warnings against such activities, rather than to understand the business process in society.

In distinction to this pathological approach, the entrepreneurial historian is interested in the culture patterns and social structures which have produced these types, in whether or not the types have been correctly delineated, and the probable influences on economic growth. In pursuing such a study, one can start with the major cultural themes that guided or sanctioned the roles of these men. About three of these there can be little controversy: the concept of the autonomous economy that was self-adjusting; the idea that progress came through competition and the survival of the fittest; and the belief that profit or material gain was the most reliable incentive for action. These themes operated throughout the society as a whole. The truckman delivering dirt for railroad construction was as much motivated by profit and as firm a believer in these themes as was the executive who was building the road. The dissident element in the society, those who denied the values of these major themes, seem during these years to have been a relatively small, or a least uninfluential, portion of the population. Therefore, if value judgments are to be formed, they should be applied to this type of society or culture. It is rather futile to assert that the culture would have been all right if it were not for the kind of people and activities that resulted directly from its major themes.

If one accepts the additional and continuing American theme that material growth is a reliable index of progress, and its usual corollary that rapid progress is desirable, one question that may be asked of the culture as a whole is whether such progress could have taken place faster if other beliefs had prevailed. Since it is impossible to conceive deductively what the United States would have been like if built up on some other system, such a decision requires the establishment of a comparative standard. But if recourse is had to the history of another nation in order to observe the application of different cultural patterns to economic development, none seems enough like the United States to offer satisfying parallels. It is interesting, however, to note that in one of the somewhat similar economic situations, that of Australia, where railroads and frontier development went on through more state enterprise, about the same things were complained of that commentators here in the United States blamed upon private enterprise. In other words, a number of the difficulties seem to have been inherent in the rapid development of a pioneer area rather than in the particular means by which the development went on.

Avoiding, therefore, such unanswerable questions, and concentrating on a better understanding of the operation of American culture, let us examine the historical conception of the "robber baron" by analyzing the history of Henry Villard. Villard is an interesting case because he was brought up outside the American culture in a German bureaucratic or official family. His father was a German lawyer and judge, who ultimately became a member of the Supreme Court of the Kingdom of Bavaria. Villard, after attendance at three European universities, decided to come to the United States and try his fortune. Supported to some extent by family money, he entered journalism and built a successful career as a correspondent for European and American newspapers. The Civil War, particularly, gave prestige to young Villard. He was able to interview Lincoln and to offer many interesting and penetrating views of contemporary events. In the early seventies he went back to Germany, and through his family connections came to know the chief financial men of Frankfort and Munich. These contacts led to his being sent over as a representative of German bondholders in the Oregon railroad and steamship enterprises that in the depression of the mid-1870's had fallen into difficulties.

It is interesting that when Villard was placed in the position of having to make judgments regarding what should be done on the unfinished Oregon and California Railroad and in regard to the Columbia River navigation projects, he readily assumed the entrepreneurial role in just about the same way as men who had been brought up in business. In other words, the entrepreneurial role seems to have been so much a part of the cultural pattern of America and possibly of middle-class Germany at this time that there was no great gulf between the attitude of the professional intellectual or journalist and that of the businessman. Villard identified himself quickly with the development of the Oregon area, and, instead of advising liquidation and withdrawal for his German clients, he counseled rather the

investment of still more capital in order to complete the enterprises. In this way his essential role was that of attracting foreign
capital to a frontier development. It is not clear that he was
ever deeply interested in problems of technology and management—that is, in just how the capital was applied for productive
purposes; rather, he became a public relations man for the area,
and an over-all or general entrepreneurial supervisor of where
the capital should be allocated.

One factor of great importance in the Villard story is that he
started new activities at just about the bottom of the deep
depression that lasted from 1873 to 1879, and his ventures from
then on, or at least from 1877 on, were first on a gradually
rising market, and finally, from 1879 to 1882, on a market that
boomed.

Villard saw quickly that the Northern Pacific Railroad, which
was being built across the country from Duluth and St. Paul,
would have to make, or at least should make, an agreement to
connect with whatever road occupied the Columbia River
valley. With this long-range plan in mind, he secured foreign
and domestic help for the building of the Oregon Railroad and
Navigation Company up the Columbia, at a time when Northern Pacific construction was moving very slowly into eastern
Montana.

It is from this point on that the most interesting differences
occur between the dramatic "robber baron" explanation of
Villard's activities and the less exciting, more socially complex
explanation offered by entrepreneurial history. The dramatic
story is that when Villard found the Northern Pacific management nearing the Columbia valley and threatening to build
either a parallel line or to cross the Cascade Mountains to
Tacoma and Seattle rather than use his facilities, he decided
to get control of the Northern Pacific. So great was his prestige
for successful operation by this time that he had the boldness
to ask a group of his friends in Wall Street to put up $8,000,000
for some project that he would not reveal to them. And, as the
story went, he had no difficulty in more than raising the first
payment requested for this "blind pool," money which he used

secretly to buy control of the Northern Pacific Railroad. The analogy is, of course, obvious and exciting. The robber baron, Villard, seizes control of a strategic pass and then exacts tribute from the railroad that represents a great, nationally subsidized enterprise.[3] Villard's blind pool has all of the trappings of high drama and shady financial dealings. The story then goes on to assert that Villard robbed the Northern Pacific and his other properties in the course of construction in such a way that by 1883 they were bankrupt, while he himself had become very rich.

Seen in broader scope, the story is not so dramatic. What appears to have happened is, that when the Northern Pacific secured Drexel Morgan financing in the latter part of the year 1880, and the Drexel Morgan-Winslow Lanier syndicate learned that Frederick Billings, the president of Northern Pacific, was planning to build duplicate facilities to the coast without regard to the already existing Oregon Railroad and Navigation Company, they became worried over the economic loss involved in constructing nearly parallel lines. The bankers, not sharing in the loyalties to individual companies that presidents and other officers almost inevitably develop, could see no reason why Northern Pacific and O.R. & N. could not get together in one cooperating line. But some of the officers of Northern Pacific, particularly Billings, regarded the railroad as their greatest life work; they felt that to compromise and make the final road a joint venture involved a personal defeat. Whereupon Morgan, at least, decided that the only way of bringing about a compromise and preventing unnecessary construction was to establish a common control for the two companies. Since Villard, who had, from the financial standpoint, acquitted himself well as receiver for Kansas Pacific, was now anxious to get this joint control, and assured Morgan that he independently had the resources to do so, the syndicate gave him their blessings, and even offered him their help. The "blind pool" was, therefore, chiefly a product of Villard's love of drama, of doing things in a spectacular fashion. Had he been willing to forgo these dra-

[3] The Northern Pacific had the largest land grant of any of the western railroads.

matic frills, control could quietly have been bought through the syndicate over about the same period. Of course, it cannot be overlooked that successfully doing the job himself gave Villard great personal prestige in Wall Street.

The difficulties from 1881 on to the completion of the road in 1883 seem to have been to some extent inevitable and to some extent to have resulted from the usual over-optimism of American promoters. Villard formed a holding company, called the Oregon and Transcontinental Company, which was to own stocks in his various enterprises, make the construction contracts, and generally conduct the building which would weld Northern Pacific and O.R. & N. into one system. Undoubtedly, the Oregon and Transcontinental Company stock was a source of large profit for Villard; in fact, it seems probable that all the money Villard made in connection with these enterprises came from floating, buying and selling the securities in Wall Street. It may be that Villard profited from the construction contracts, but there is no clear evidence of this, and it is quite possible, by analogy to similar situations, that the profits of construction went largely to local contractors in the West. At all events, the major difficulty was lack of sufficient traffic to warrant the high construction cost of building railroads through the Rockies and the Oregon coastal regions. The completion of the through-line in August of 1883 was almost simultaneous with the beginning of a steady recession in general business that ended in a crisis the following March. As a result, the difficulties that the system would have experienced in paying returns under any circumstances were accentuated. When the companies were not able to pay dividends and their securities declined, Villard, temporarily losing the confidence of the banking syndicate, was forced to retire from the control of the various enterprises.

One way, therefore, of looking at this whole story is that Villard, a relatively inexperienced entrepreneur, took hold of a series of frontier developments at the bottom of the business cycle, carried them along, through his connections and personal enthusiasm, during the rise of the cycle, completed them just at the peak of the boom, and was then unable to steer them through the ensuing depression. Viewed from this angle, the whole development was a normal and repetitive one in both big and small business. The general history of even a small retail store or factory enterprise was often just about the same; if the enterprise started at a favorable time in the business cycle, it could last until a major depression. Then, unless it had had farsighted and unusually able management, or had been lucky in making more profit than was possible for most young enterprises, it lapsed into bankruptcy and had to be reorganized with the injection of new capital. The roles that Villard played extremely well were those of a mobilizer of capital resources for pioneer investments, and effective public relations for the development of an area. The roles that he played poorly were those of an expert railroad builder and conservative business forecaster.

What do entrepreneurial historians expect to gain from such a study? In the first place, the study of outstanding examples such as that of Villard may be instructive for the study of the normal practices and operations of business. A detailed study of the Villard enterprises will show more exactly the strategic type of entrepreneurship that went into railroad building. The seizing of the transportation route down the Columbia River is merely a dramatic example of the general type of planning done by all western railroad builders. The strategic occupation of territory was like a great game of chess. Each leading entrepreneur had to guess where his rivals were likely to build next, how he could forestall their entrance into an area by throwing a line of track through some valley or across some river, often planning these moves a decade or more ahead. Little is known of the local economic and social results of this process beyond the fact that it extended railroad transportation at an extremely rapid rate.

Trying to assess the larger economic and social effects of Villard's activities, we might note that he mobilized about $60,000,000 in capital, and applied it to western development at a social cost of perhaps one or two million dollars. That is,

he may have made more money than that, but the one or two
million dollars represent an estimate of what he actually spent
on living and personal durable goods in these years. His other
money came and went in stockmarket operations, and presumably represented a transfer of capital from one set of holders
to another. The question remains: granting that this was not
a high rate of commission to pay for the mobilization of so much
money, was the long-run effect of the development for which
the money was spent economically and socially desirable? Undoubtedly, this particular development of transportation was
premature, and it was carried on at the cost of some other types
of goods or services that could have been produced with the
same expenditure. But this in turn raises another question from
a purely nationalistic standpoint: could the foreign capital have
been attracted for more prosaic and routine operations? To
the extent that foreign money was invested unprofitably in
western development, it was an economic loss to Germany and
the other investing nations, but a net gain to the United States.
As to the loss of domestic resources in these developments, it
can be noted that, at least, this is what the men of the culture
apparently wanted to do with their economic energy. Villard
noted in his promotion activities that the word "Oregon" had
a kind of popular magic to it in the seventies and early eighties.
Then it was the promised land of the American West, and it
stimulated the imagination of Americans along entrepreneurial
lines. The historian should try to assess the extent to which the
dramatic development of natural resources may actually raise
the rate of saving in the community, and may increase output
of energy in the population as a whole. These are, of course,
very difficult and intangible problems, yet they are just as much
a part of the picture of economic development as the old stand-
by of assessing the value of natural resources and the cost of
getting them to market.

There is a cultural paradox involved in all of this that makes
it difficult for the unwary investigator. At the same time that
Americans were saving at a high rate for development purposes
and investing in railroad securities, they had a distrust of the

railroad operator and were inclined to make the railroads a scapegoat for many of their ills. In other words, there was a kind of national Manicheaen heresy, whereby, people were willing to sell themselves to the devil, to worship evil, as it were, but at the same time were not ready to forget the fact that it was really the devil and not good that they were supporting. This whole problem of ambiguity of attitude toward business leaders, and the reactions it led to on the part of the executives themselves, is one of the fruitful fields of American cultural history.

Consideration of public opinion leads directly to the problem of social sanctions: what codes of conduct, ethics, mores, and folkways were recognized by the railroad entrepreneur? The robber-baron approach has implied that there were few sanctions recognized, that these men operated on the basis of nearly complete expediency. To anyone familiar with the study of cultures, this is obviously a very questionable assertion. Actually, there were many but varying sanctions operative upon the business leaders of the period. These varied with: types of activity, horse-trading, for instance, having one set of ethics, banking quite another; the conditioning of the entrepreneur, whereby a man brought up in the strict and staid business community of Philadelphia would have ethics different from one brought up in a less rigidly structured society; and the geographic region, the frontier, in general, being an area of greater opportunity and larger adherence to the "end-justifies-the-means" philosophy than more settled areas, the mining town of Virginia City and Boston perhaps illustrating extreme poles.

Let us take a particular type of social sanction and see how it operated on the basis of these differing situations. One of the most important ones was the feeling of a fiduciary obligation toward stockholders and bondholders—the recognition of the fact that managers were trustees for the real owners of the property. From this standpoint, the distinction between men and regions may be brought out by analyzing the promotion of an extension up the Mississippi River by the directors of the Chicago, Burlington & Quincy Railroad.

But before proceeding to the details of these operations, it is necessary to understand some of the culture patterns of pioneer development and railroad building. The ultimate growth and welfare of the community was a rationalization that to the Westerner justified almost any means that he might employ, particularly in the handling of Easterners' capital. Added to this was the fact that railroad companies were not equipped to do their own construction work and had to let local contractors do the building. That the construction work was not done by contract simply to rob the stockholders is abundantly illustrated by the facts that the most mature and best-managed companies continued to build through contractors, even though they might have set-up departments to do the work themselves, and that railroad contractors sometimes bankrupted themselves by bidding too low. The difficulties were that building was a specialized enterprise for which the railroad had no regular staff, that for any one railroad it was occasional rather than continuous and, therefore, did not justify the maintenance of a specialized staff, and that usually the work was remote from the railroad offices and could not readily be supervised by the chief executives. In order to facilitate such large-scale work by local interests, it would often be necessary for the road itself, or the directors or large stockholders of the road, to put up cash to assist the local contractor. This would be done by buying stock in a construction company of which the operating executive would usually be a local builder. The construction company took its pay in railroad stocks or bonds, which might in the case of an old road be almost as good as cash, but in the case of many young roads might be of very speculative and dubious value. The par value of securities taken for construction work, therefore, is not a safe guide to the amount of profit actually realized by construction companies. But there is little question that a great deal of eastern stockholders' money went west into construction companies and stayed there as profit to local entrepreneurs, including subcontractors all the way down the line, and even to the owners of local sandbanks and hardware stores. Sometimes the eastern directors and stockholders who had advanced money for construction company stock made handsome profits; at other times, as in the case to be discussed, they lost what they had put in; but in any case, the local people were likely to make a profit. As John Murray Forbes, Boston railroad promoter and conservative financier, put it, "My feeling is . . . that the Landowners and R. Road contractors are the ones who too often get the whole benefit of the money that Capitalists put into the West."[4] Charles E. Perkins, long-time president of the C.B. & Q. went even further: "Iowa people make more money in farms and other industries including contracting and building than in railroads . . . and it is only the eastern capitalist who cannot use his money to advantage at home who is willing to risk it in western railroads and take the low average return which he gets, a return very much lower than the average of other investments in this state [of Iowa]."[5]

This background is necessary to an understanding of the contracts for the so-called River Roads that were to go up the Mississippi from Clinton, Iowa, ultimately to Minneapolis and St. Paul. The central western city involved in this development was Dubuque, Iowa, and the local entrepreneur who undertook to do the construction was J. K. Graves. He was a small-scale general entrepreneur interested in banking, building, and all the wide range of local enterprises usual to the small-city capitalist. In order to undertake construction on these roads, he persuaded a group of the C.B. & Q. directors, headed by ex-president James F. Joy, to put up about half a million dollars cash in return for securities of the construction company. They then entered into a contract with the two railroad companies that were to own and operate the lines after they had been built, whereby the construction company took pay partly in stocks and bonds. The rest of the bonds of these companies were to be marketed to the holders of C.B. & Q. bonds and stock, who would buy them readily because of the endorsement of

[4] John Murray Forbes to Charles S. Tuckerman, Apr. 14, 1880. President's Letters (Chicago: Burlington & Quincy Archives, Newberry Library).
[5] Charles E. Perkins to James W. McDill, Jan. 26, 1885. President's Letters (Chicago: Burlington & Quincy Archives, Newberry Library) .

their own directors; this would in turn provide additional capital that could be used to pay for the construction.

Some of the members of the C.B. & Q. board, particularly John Murray Forbes and J. N. A. Griswold, were not told at the time they endorsed the sale of the bonds that their fellow directors were actually interested in the stock of the construction company. It seems probable that this knowledge was withheld because Joy and the directors who did buy such stock recognized that Forbes would not approve of their being involved in this kind of relationship. In other words, there appears to have been a difference in the business morality or sanctions recognized by James F. Joy, a western businessman, and those recognized by old, conservative, upper-class Easterners like Forbes and Griswold.

The working out of the pattern has much in common with the Villard story. Graves may or may not have been a good railroad builder; examination of hundreds of letters to and from Graves, and letters discussing the situation among C.B. & Q. directors, has failed to provide conclusive information on this point. At least, he held the confidence of Joy and the other interested directors right up to the final failure of the enterprise. The contracts were let in the boom of 1871, and, when the depression hit after the panic of 1873, the roads had not been completed. With revenues of all kinds falling off, Graves started borrowing from the funds of the unfinished River Roads to support his other local enterprises. The result was a slowing down of construction, a default on the bonds of the River Roads, and a financial situation that would not bear close scrutiny by accountants. In all this it is very hard to pass moral judgments. Graves had undoubtedly thought that he was doing the best thing possible for Dubuque and the surrounding country by trying to build up many enterprises at once. He had made no plans for a break in the boom and the coming of depression. As a result, he found himself hopelessly involved in ventures that could not all be kept going; yet the abandonment of any one of them then meant a postponing of all or most of the benefit that was expected to accrue from it. In this situation he tried to borrow from Peter to pay Paul, hoping that Peter would raise additional funds. The same kind of situation has turned pillars of society into scoundrels time and time again in American business history.

In the case of the River Roads, when the default occurred, Forbes and Griswold became interested in investigating the situation and soon found out the identity of the construction company's stockholders and the nature of the contracts. Forbes denounced Joy, and when the latter refused to assume personal responsibility to the C.B. & Q. investors for the interest in the River Road bonds—a procedure which would have been highly unusual—Forbes decided that Joy and certain other directors involved must be put off the C.B. & Q. board. Forbes succeeded in doing this in a proxy battle at the next stockholders' meeting and the River Roads passed ultimately into the hands of the Chicago, Milwaukee and St. Paul. This, in the long run, turned out to be a great mistake, as a decade later C.B. & Q. had to build a parallel line under less advantageous circumstances.

The quarrel was due to a conflict in sanctions based upon differences in situation. As one of Joy's followers in the matter, John W. Brooks, C.B. & Q. director who had had much experience in the West, put it, "Loosely as these things were done [branch-line contracts and construction in general] they as a whole have proved the salvation of the C.B. & Q. . . . we do not claim to be immaculate beyond expediency, but are content with right intentions and the good results obtained on the whole. . . ."[6]

Perhaps the above examples have demonstrated the difficulty in condemning any particular group of business leaders without careful analysis of the situation involved, the popular and local codes of ethics, and the general pressure for "justification by profit" that ran all through American culture.

These illustrations have shown only limited aspects of entrepreneurial history. They have touched on, but not elaborated, the political science of the business corporation and the analysis

[6] John W. Brooks to James F. Joy, Mar. 11, 1875. Joy Collection (Ann Arbor, Michigan: Michigan Historical Collections).

of power within the corporation, showing only in the latter case that it is not easy to put one's finger on the exact location of control in any given instance. Real control over a situation may rest with some contractor or underling in the West, despite the facade of power in the eastern executive officers. Many other relations have not been brought out at all in these two accounts, for example, the relation of business roles to other social roles, which carries with it the discussion of the role of the business elite in relation to cultural leadership. Many railroad men were active leaders in national or state politics; others were patrons of the arts, or supporters of education. To what extent were these attitudes outgrowths of general social mores, to what extent did business sanctions indicate that these supplementary roles should be played, and to what extent were they peculiarities of the individuals?

Comparative studies need to be made of the place of entrepreneurship in varying national cultures. There seems little doubt that such studies will go further toward explaining the economic progress of different regions than will any assessment of potential natural resources. It is these cultural elements that determine, to a very large degree, who will become entrepreneurs (the quantity and quality of the supply of entrepreneurship), and also the likelihood of entrepreneurial success in various types of endeavor. A culture with feudal standards of lavish living or the support of elaborate ceremonial organizations of church and state will obviously not have the capital to invest in economic development that will be available in a culture where frugal living, saving, and work are the custom.

The resources of the social sciences may be applied more readily to historical problems in the study of special roles and functions, such as entrepreneurship, than in the general study of the enormous conventional fields of economic, social, political or intellectual history. To learn more about how human beings behave and have behaved in history, it is wise to start with a manageable and definable group of human beings performing certain functions, rather than with the activities of the society as a whole.

V: The Entrepreneur in
American Capital Formation[*]

To distinguish the element of entrepreneurship in capital
formation it may be permissible to divide the factors that produce commercially usable credit into those dependent on the
general culture and those directly responsive to entrepreneurial
activity. Such a division must be seen simply as a heuristic
device, since entrepreneurship itself is part of the general culture, and habits of saving are no doubt altered by the returns
on investment. But from the standpoint of this artificial division
we may say that Americans had certain propensities to save, not
directly the product of contemporary entrepreneurial activity,
and that the creative role of the entrepreneur in capital formation was to mobilize existing savings, supply incentives for a
higher rate of saving, utilize credit mechanisms that could lead
to forced saving, and achieve productivity from the use of capital
that would add to the national income and particularly to the
supply of business savings. There are at least two types of entrepreneurial functions involved in the performance of this highly
generalized role: those of the entrepreneur who acquires, allo-
cates, and manages capital for actual production; and those of
the financial agent who develops ways of raising capital for the
use of others.

* Reprinted with permission from: National Bureau of Economic Research Universities—National Bureau Committee for Economic Growth,
Capital Formation and Economic Growth (Princeton, 1956). The author is
indebted for suggestions and criticisms to Arthur H. Cole, Leland H. Jenks,
and others at the Research Center for Entrepreneurial History at Harvard;
and also to Moses Abramovitz, Simon Kuznets, and Harold F. Williamson.

71

If history is to make its maximum contribution to any current problem it is usually necessary to go back to proximate origins and see existing institutions in earlier and simpler forms. The historian sees the activities of the big business manager of the twentieth century emerging from those of the industrial entrepreneur of the nineteenth, and these in turn against the background of earlier American agricultural and commercial culture. The historical technique gains in utility for present world problems from the fact that in relation to Great Britain the United States up to about 1850 was an underdeveloped area.[1]

I

It is obvious from a cursory view of United States history that nineteenth century entrepreneurs represented a high level of business energy. Statistical series document the rapid growth of American business and productivity, particularly during the nineteenth century. Of fundamental importance to an understanding of this period of tremendous growth is the background of American Colonial culture. In the beginning Americans had come from the already economically well-developed nations of Western Europe. The immigrants to America were from Great Britain, Holland, Germany, France, and Sweden, where, either in rural or urban areas, they had in general been in contact with fairly advanced stages of trade and handicraft. Unlike the people of most underdeveloped areas today, these migrants had value systems already adjusted to capitalist needs and goals. The fact that the two early American colonizing agencies were companies designed to return profits to stockholders gave a business atmosphere to problems of settlement.[2]

To a greater degree than the European population as a whole, the migrants represented heterodox minorities conditioned to

[1] This paper was written before the research for *The Puerto Rican Businessman,* and *Entrepreneurship in Argentine Culture,* hence there are no Latin American comparisons.

[2] See Wesley F. Craven, *Dissolution of the Virginia Company* (Oxford, Eng.: Oxford University Press, 1932).

searching for new ways of coping with their social and physical environment. In this country, Europeans found communities with relatively low man-land ratios and almost unlimited opportunity for increasing returns from the application of labor either to agriculture or industry. As a result, a premium was placed on putting to use devices or methods that would save man-hours, regardless of their efficiency in relation to physical resources.

To some extent Colonial society reproduced European feudal patterns and recognized class distinctions, but barriers to social mobility were relatively weak. The early comers, who presumably did much to set colonial culture patterns, were conditioned by the needs of relatively open-class pioneer communities. There was no great difficulty in achieving high social prestige through the acquisition of property within a man's own lifetime.[3] The fact that it was possible for any intelligent man to get ahead, no doubt created an attitude of competitiveness, or what has later been called a class-status-prestige complex, stronger than that of the nonmigrating English or Continental peoples. Aside from business, including commercial farming, the avenues to social prestige were relatively few and unrewarding. The salaried positions in the army and navy were held by British officers merely stationed here for a brief period. Similarly the highest offices of government were of British appointment and the church had no Colonial hierarchy that led to such posts as canon, dean, and bishop. In the later years of colonial development there were relatively fewer opportunities to gain rapid wealth from the land. Thus trade and manufacturing necessarily became chosen avenues for social mobility.

Elements favorable to entrepreneurial activity appear to have resulted from the loose integration of American culture. Patterns disrupted by transplantation and to a lesser extent by competition with those of other cultures did not resume their old depth

[3] See W. T. Baxter, *The House of Hancock* (Cambridge: Harvard University Press, 1945); and James B. Hedges, *The Browns of Providence Plantations* (Cambridge: Harvard University Press, 1952). Although Baxter is a professor of accounting, neither book has a satisfactory analysis of capital accounts. Merchants did not balance their books with a view to determining net worth.

or fixity. This meant that the entrepreneur could restructure the culture more nearly to suit his needs. Ralph Linton, for example, has written of the innovator as a deviant personality in terms of deeply patterned cultures.[4] This was not necessarily the case in the United States. Since new environments and new possibilities in transportation continuously forced change, innovators may well have had personalities that could be called normal to the culture.[5] In fact, if one uses the term broadly to indicate new methods not previously practiced by the particular group, innovation must have been frequent, once a certain stage of development was reached in the new American areas.[6]

Another factor favorable to the prestige and success of the entrepreneur was the lack of established leadership in new communities. The local merchant or manufacturer might readily occupy the power vacuum which existed because of the lack of well-established leading landowners and politically prominent families, such as characterized old settlements.

As business success came increasingly to be the avenue to social prestige, a large supply of men was available for entrepreneurial pursuits. In addition, many occupations that in a foreign nation would not have been regarded as entrepreneurial or conducive to innovation or expansion in capital investment turned out to be such in the United States. For example, an able man keeping a general store in a growing part of the United States usually had an eye on every local opportunity. As soon as he made a little money in the store, he spread out into other local enterprises and became, in a sense, a small-scale general entrepreneur. In good times, college professors, doctors, and lawyers all joined

[4] In *The Progress of Underdeveloped Areas*, Bert F. Hoselitz (Chicago: University of Chicago Press, 1952), p. 75.

[5] There has been no historical study of personality types per se. This supposition might be tested from the many biographies, collected letters, and autobiographies of businessmen of the early nineteenth century. See Henrietta M. Larson, *Guide to Business History* (Cambridge: Harvard University Press, 1948).

[6] Modifying this is the fact that frontier communities with their cooperative labor practices tended to standardize procedures. See Donald McConnell, *Economic Virtues in the United States* (published by author, 1930), pp. 12 ff.

in the scramble for wealth from the profitable allocation of capital.

Lewis Atherton's studies indicate the high social prestige and the subsidiary enterprises of general storekeepers even in the relatively static Deep South.

Here there was a tendency to develop a position of great influence. While this was primarily economic in nature, it also frequently expressed itself in political terms. At least one storekeeper was generally to be found on city councils, and frequently the majority came from that occupation. Self-interest of course made the work attractive. When municipal ordinances covered mercantile and peddling licenses, rates of drayage and the speed at which drays could travel, business hours, rules for the city market, inspection of weights and measures, fire regulations, and similar objects, it behooved a storekeeper to exert himself to obtain an opportunity to participate in making the decisions. . . .

He served as a middleman between seaboard wholesalers and southern farmers, thus handling the generous and long-range credit which characterized the system. He bartered merchandise for farm crops, and by marketing the latter offered an outlet for southern farms.

In the process of providing these basic economic services the storekeeper naturally contributed to other economic and social activities as well. In processing farm crops for market he provided an elementary type of manufacturing by operating subsidiary enterprises such as sawmills and gristmills. Banking, farming, transportation, and land speculation were all so closely related to his scheme of operation that he had to deal with the problems involved in each. Moreover, storekeepers constituted the central group in the development of interior villages and towns in the ante-bellum period.[7]

America has also had subcultures with different sets of values. These have ranged from that of back-country people who had much of the cultural outlook of the Middle Ages still intact to the progressive business culture along the northeastern seaboard. In this latter culture frugality and saving were seen not only as manifestations of a proper life, but also as a means for acquiring more economic power that could be used for God's work. A for-

[7] Lewis E. Atherton, *The Southern Country* (Baton Rouge, La.: Louisiana State University Press, 1949), pp. 191-193. Quoted by permission. See also his *The Pioneer Merchant in Mid-America* (University of Missouri Press, 1939).

eigner viewing this segment of the culture in 1836 wrote, "There is, probably, no people on earth with whom business constitutes pleasure, and industry amusement, in an equal degree with the inhabitants of the United States of America."[8] These were the proper values for entrepreneurship and rapid capital formation. When carried westward by merchants, teachers, skilled workers, and transportation executives this "puritan" subculture came to dominate most of the nation.[9]

Another set of general conditioning factors is connected with the rapid geographical and demographical expansion in the eighteenth and nineteenth centuries. A high reproduction rate insured an expanding local population in almost every settled area. In addition to this, young men born in the country were continually migrating to towns and cities, giving vitality and innovating impulses to those growing centers. Immigration from abroad also was rapid after 1845. These factors meant that, aside from a few declining agricultural areas in the East, a business started in almost any community would grow if it merely held its competitive position. The usual western promoter would have agreed with J. W. Smith of Hudson, Ohio that it was safe continually to add new business ventures, since as the town grew each would "support the other."[10]

[8] F. J. Grund, *The Americans* (London, 1837), Vol. 2, p. 202. There is a voluminous literature of accounts by foreign travelers from which the characteristics of American culture might be reconstructed in a systematic way. Hunt's *Merchants Magazine, De Bow's Review,* and the *Banker's Magazine* also contain articles on American business practices written by foreign (usually British) businessmen.

[9] McConnell's *Economic Virtues in the United States,* as cited, repays reading in this connection.

[10] William Miller, ed., *Men in Business* (Cambridge: Harvard University Press, 1952; New York: Harper Torchbooks edition, 1961), p. 187. This situation is indicated in the early pages of city and county histories. I found it to be the case with most successful local brewers. It is indicated in my *The Pabst Brewing Company* (New York: New York University Press, 1948), but since Pabst was selling in the national market, expansion by reinvestment in the company was more attractive than in the case of the local brewery. Therefore, general investment activity came at a later stage in the career of Frederick Pabst.

II

In the early phase of industrialization most initial financing was of local origin and there was an intimate relation between entrepreneurs and investors. Expansion of the business was usually financed by reinvesting profits. In this way the efficiency of the entrepreneur as a manager had a direct bearing upon the rate of capital formation. Harold F. Williamson has suggested that the desire to exercise control over invested capital may have led entrepreneurs to favor reinvestment of earnings in their own firms rather than in more productive outside activities. In addition, the effort to compensate for scarce labor by using more machinery led to a continual demand for additional capital equipment.

The rise of large-scale transportation and public utility enterprises from about 1820 on emphasized new methods of finance such as widespread sale of securities and creation of bank credit. The first method raised the problems of entrepreneurial capital obtained from investors who lacked intimate knowledge of the properties named on their certificates of ownership, often the money was raised by impersonal appeals in one section of the country for investment in another.

Much ingenuity was required to raise enough capital to build cities and railroads at the rates that prevailed from 1830 to 1860. The population in cities over 8,000 increased from 4.9 per cent of the total in 1820 to 16.1 per cent in 1860, and the number of such cities from 13 to 141. From 1836 until the late 1840's, depression and debt repudiations retarded the raising of capital for railroad construction, but in the decade of the 1850's the United States laid down more than 20,000 miles of track.

Capital for these ventures was raised by a series of devices in which the role of entrepreneurship is often hard to distinguish from that of government responding to public pressure. The means represented a mixture of techniques both borrowed from Europe and originated in the United States. First, commercial banks bought stocks for their portfolios.[11] On occasion, states forced banks to invest in internal improvements in order to gain renewal of their charters. Second, commercial banks extended renewable loans or demand loans secured by stock to various business enterprises, particularly railroads, loans that became in effect a part of the capital structure of the road, and were ultimately paid off from the sale of securities. Third, development banks were chartered by the states for the express purpose of issuing notes that could be used to build internal improvements, and occasionally, railroad companies were granted banking privileges to enable them to issue their own notes. Fourth, real estate companies were associated regularly with the construction of railroads and often with the starting of factories.[12] Since the improvement projected promised an almost certain rise in surrounding land values, large investors could be forced to buy stock in the railroad or manufacturing company in order to be included in the land company.[13] Fifth, construction companies, again promising a more certain and immediate return than the improvement that was being constructed, could often raise equity capital or loans when the transportation company could not. Sixth, state and local governments put up large sums for the purchase of railroad and canal securities, generally through the sale of their own bonds, and insofar as these investments were not serviced by the improvement company the burden was borne by taxation.[14] Seventh, entrepreneurs also persuaded some of the

[11] For material on this and other aspects of the mechanics of investment in the nineteenth century see Fritz Redlich, *The Moulding of American Banking*, 2 vols. (Hafner, 1951). His book contains the only adequate account of the rise of investment banking.

[12] For examples of real estate companies in manufacturing finance see George S. Gibb, *The Whitesmiths of Taunton* (Cambridge: Harvard University Press, 1943) ; and Charles W. Moore, *Timing a Century* (Cambridge: Harvard University Press, 1945), both in the Harvard Studies in Business History.

[13] There is plenty of material on railroad finance and promotion and the early history of railroad companies; for an introduction, see Frederick A. Cleveland and Fred W. Powell, *Railroad Promotion and Capitalization in the United States* (Longmans, 1909); and Carter Goodrich, *Government Promotion of American Canals and Railroads, 1800-1890* (New York: Columbia University Press, 1960).

[14] Harry M. Pierce contends that when governments invested in railroad securities at prices that could not have been obtained in the open market, the difference between the government and the market price was a subsidy.

states, such as Georgia, Pennsylvania, and New York, to build major railroads or canals at state expense.[15]

In this broad capital-raising process the difficulty in distinguishing between general cultural factors and those specifically connected with the pattern of entrepreneurship becomes obvious. One might say it was an entrepreneurial culture. In fact, it is hard to distinguish between entrepreneurs and the rest of the population. From the demands of their function, the entrepreneurs were presumably the men of energy and imagination along these material lines, and they educated the rest. The rise of a belief in material progress and of a willingness to make present sacrifices for future material rewards has been going on since the colonial period.

The economic returns from improved transportation were so high and widespread, particularly in interior communities previously cut off from markets, that such improvements became a major goal.[16] Local people were ready to make sacrifices to secure transportation and dreamed of benefits that far exceeded the ultimate reality. The people of Oswego, New York, for example, were said to be "unanimous for anything in the form of a railroad whether it goes crooked or straight they seem to have no care."[17] When the capital required exceeded that which could be raised by local entrepreneurs, they joined with investors in efforts to secure state aid.

Between 1835 and 1840 Illinois illustrated the excessive public

Railroads of New York: A Study of Government Aid, 1826-1875 (Cambridge: Harvard University Press, 1953), pp. 20-21. See also Goodrich, *Government Promotion;* Milton Heath, *Constructive Liberalism* (Cambridge: Harvard University Press, 1954); Oscar and Mary F. Handlin, *Commonwealth* (New York: New York University Press, 1947); and Louis Hartz, *Economic Policy and Democratic Thought* (Cambridge: Harvard University Press, 1948).

[15] See Julius Rubin, *Canal or Railroad: Imitation and Innovation in the Response to the Erie Canal in Philadelphia, Baltimore and Boston,* Transactions of the American Philosophical Society, New Series v. 51, pt. 3, 1961. There was also some financing of internal improvements by lotteries. See H. J. G. Aitken, "Yates and McIntyre: Lottery Managers," *The Journal of Economic History,* Winter 1953, pp. 36-57.

[16] See Leland H. Jenks, "Railroads as an Economic Force," *The Journal of Economic History,* May 1944, pp. 1-21.

[17] Pierce, *Railroads of New York,* p. 42.

investment in a frontier area produced by a combination of popular demand, persuasive entrepreneurs, and a great boom period.[18] Encouraged by a federal land grant of 290,914 acres, the
legislature in 1835 authorized a $500,000 bond issue to finance a
canal between Lake Michigan and the Illinois River. As security
for the bonds, the state pledged the federal land and the canal
tolls. But this was only a beginning. The full force of the boom
psychology struck the state in 1836 and 1837. Land near the Chicago end of the canal which had remained unsold at $1.25 an
acre less than ten years before now sold as high as $20,000 for a
building lot. Caught in the excitement of the early months of
1837, the legislature established a comprehensive system of internal improvements. Seven railroads were to be built at once, each
starting from an intersection with a navigable river, and construction work was to progress simultaneously in both directions!
Navigation of the major rivers within the state was to be improved, and $200,000 was earmarked for compensation to coun-
ties in which no railroad or river improvements took place. An
issue of $8,000,000 in 6 per cent bonds, salable only at par or
above, was provided to pay for the state system. Needless to add,
the depression which commenced in mid-1837 resulted in abandonment of most of the work and default on the bonds. Between
1830 and 1890 each new tier of western states went through such
periods of over-optimism and over-investment, and private enterprise followed the same pattern. R. Richard Wohl has written a
case history showing a boom-time pattern of mid-nineteenth century private investment.[19] His account is especially interesting
because it illustrates the tendency of the optimistic business atmosphere to turn American professional men into entrepreneurs.
Wohl's leading figure, Henry Noble Day, was a professor in the
Western Reserve Theological Department at Hudson, Ohio to
whom the boom of the early 1850's brought dreams that his village would become a great railroad center. Day's conversion to
business life was aided by the fact that education did not share

[18] See Reginald C. McGrane, *Foreign Bondholders and American State
Debts* (New York: The Macmillan Co., 1935) , pp. 102 ff.
[19] R. Richard Wohl, "Henry Noble Day," in *Men in Business*, William
Miller, ed., pp. 178-188, passim. Quoted by permission.

in the flush times. The closing of the Theological Department in 1850 just as the railroad from Cleveland was nearing Hudson ended Day's teaching. He justified his transition to full-time entrepreneur in Calvinistic terms: "The characteristics which Christianity in its present stage seems to require are chiefly vigor of invention, skill in execution and subscribing to the true end of industrial arts—utility."

As in most western towns the railroad seemed the key to unlimited prosperity. Before the Cleveland and Pittsburgh even reached Hudson and years before any through connection to the East, Day was chartering branch lines and planning a transcontinental system through the town.

But for Henry Day himself the dream he had for Hudson had become a sacred reality. He was able to anticipate its completion when the first few spadefuls of earth were taken out for grading. He proceeded therefore to enact the logic of his expectations. He began to create a network of businesses in Hudson to service the demands arising out of the railroad building boom and to cash in on the enlarged market which would result once the roads were completed. . . .

In 1849, Henry Day began what was to be the seat of nearly a dozen separate businesses. That year he approached Western Reserve College for a loan of $1,500 with which he would undertake to construct a large commercial building. Since the railroad was to come shortly to Hudson, there would be a great demand for business floor space, of which there was hardly any available in the town. Against the loan he would pledge the lot on which he intended to erect the structure. In addition, he would pay the going rate of interest and retire the loan as rapidly as he could.

No sooner had he begun the actual building when his plans for the structure were enlarged into something far grander. Less than a year later, the [un]completed building had exceeded its planned cost of $3,000. . . . Before the structure was completed to his satisfaction it had swallowed up $18,000 although the source of this capital remains to this day a mystery which cannot be solved from the tangled, incestuous financing which prevailed in Henry Day's enterprises.

The structure was a magnificent aberration, entirely out of scale with the relatively small, low buildings which filled the rest of the village. It was a five-sided, three-story edifice—an earlier Pentagon—and was soon packed full of a collection of businesses at the bottom of each of which was Henry Day, impartially providing capital, plans, and enthusiasm. . . .

In the meantime the projected railroads brought a great stream of cash and hundreds of workers into Hudson. Of the $200,000 pledged for the Clinton Railroad, $18,000 was expended within Hudson itself, a proportion far greater than it appears, since many of the subscriptions to stock were made in the form of lands, not cash. The numerical expansion of the population also created a host of new problems which boomed business. The greatest demand was for shelter and Henry Day proposed to meet it with a vertically integrated scheme for new housing.

One of the greatest benefits of the railroad boom, its protagonist argued, was to be the enhancement of local land values. Hence Henry Day, associating himself with the most powerful elements in the community, purchased—on credit of course—large tracts of land outside the main area of settlement in the town, but immediately adjacent to it. Here—in what he labeled "Day's Addition"—he proposed to rear the housing which was to accommodate the present increase in population as well as the further additions which would surely come after the railroads were fully built. To finance construction and sale of his houses, Day conceived a special kind of banking organization, the "Hudson Society for Savings."

The main sources of capital for the Day companies were the enterprises of his relatives. He drew on the working capital of New York and southern trading and banking companies and on family wealth accumulated from earlier mercantile ventures in the East. In this way eastern credit was stretched to the utmost for Ohio improvements. The result, as in many similar instances, was collapse of the whole structure in the business recession of 1854.

In Day's case and many others, including some state-financed ventures, most or a large part of the capital prematurely invested was lost. The railroad culverts melted away as farmers "borrowed" the stones, and the grading reverted to humps in the pastureland. But there were nearly similar cases where the bad initial estimates, the "entrepreneurial errors," as John E. Sawyer has called them, led to the construction of ultimately valuable works that would not have been undertaken or continued had the true costs and difficulties been known in advance or at an early stage. Sawyer writes that "Once in operation, to fit our conditions the project must have proved, according to the definition chosen, such a contribution to the economic development of the community or such a source of profits to its owners—as to have more than justified the total cost. That it paid off in any form means, of course, that the error in estimating costs was at least offset by a corresponding error in the estimation of demand."[20]

He cites as well-known instances the Welland and Middlesex Canals, the Hoosac Tunnel, and the building of Sault Ste. Marie, Michigan. In the latter case Francis H. Clergue built an industrial community with power, pulp and other mills, machine shops, foundries, nickel mines, iron mines, railroads, charcoal kilns, and finally a large-scale steel industry in advance of any local or otherwise established demand. Sawyer concludes:

Here capital was progressively, and more and more unwillingly, poured into a lasting exercise in economic development that proved a near miss from the point of view of its investors; but which was then so far under way that the 'high social cost of abandonment' enabled it to command transitional public funds when crisis came to the over-extended empire.

As the foregoing examples have illustrated, acute scarcity of local capital in western communities did not prevent the coming into being of an excess of capital equipment. In the upswings of the business cycle there was a continuous trend toward over-expansion. Business buildings were bigger and more numerous than the trade warranted, railroads were built ahead of traffic, and factories were started before there was an adequate market. The successful local man would likely engage in more enterprises than he could effectively manage. But such excessive activity led to a continuous movement of workers, either manual or white-collar, into the entrepreneurial ranks. This, in turn, meant that entrepreneurs were recruited from a very large percentage of the total population and that there was a steadily large movement into and out of entrepreneurial activities.

[20] John E. Sawyer, "Entrepreneurial Error and Economic Growth," in *Explorations in Economic History,* May 1952, pp. 200 and pp. 203-204. Quoted by permission.

Vigorous individual entrepreneurship may necessarily involve a high ratio of miscalculation and failure, a high ratio of entries and exits. American entrepreneurs like R. H. Macy and Cyrus McCormick failed in their early ventures, and many successful companies have been through one or more bankruptcies. Managerial know-how, essential to ultimate capital formation, was learned at the expense of empty-handed creditors.

III

It has seemed convenient to refer to the men who organized and controlled multifarious enterprises as general entrepreneurs. The criterion being that the man should not immerse himself in the details of management of any single enterprise, but that alone or in cooperation with similar operators he should control a number of enterprises in diverse, but not necessarily unrelated, lines of business. A man like Erastus Corning of Albany traded in hardware, manufactured iron, controlled railroads, and was president of a bank that supplied credit for such enterprises.[21]

General entrepreneurs operating regionally or locally formed an important link between the creation of credit and productive enterprise. As presidents or directors of banks they were in favored positions for negotiating loans. Sometimes "secured" by the stock of the enterprise involved, more often merely by one- or two-name paper, bank loans were frequently the source of both fixed and working capital. During boom periods the imaginative ventures of these entrepreneurs undoubtedly drew bank credit far in excess of local savings into long-term construction,[22] and by the resulting inflation taxed the rest of the community for the benefit of faster capital formation.

By the same mixture of enthusiasm and ability, entrepreneurs in control of large ventures drew upon the capital resources of Europe. This took place in two ways. First, since men like Cor-

[21] Irene Neu, *Erastus Corning: Merchant and Financier, 1794-1872* (Ithaca: Cornell University Press, 1960).

[22] Jenks, "Railroads as an Economic Force." See also his *The Migration of British Capital to 1875* (New York: Alfred E. Knopf, 1927).

nelius Vanderbilt, Henry Villard, Nathaniel Thayer, or John Murray Forbes were known to foreign bankers, their participation in a venture was a sufficient guarantee to attract foreign capital.[23] Second, these men and their companies advertised the West and its farming land. This attracted immigrants with capital in cash or skill.[24] At the least, the economy gained an able-bodied adult worker without having to pay for his upbringing. At the most, the economy might gain the transplantation of a going enterprise, either agricultural or industrial, from Europe to America. For example, the Bests who started the Pabst Brewery moved their business from Mettenheim in the Rheinish Palatinate by selling their brewery, and building a new one with the proceeds in Milwaukee, Wisconsin.[25]

The general entrepreneurs played a major role in reshaping the American environment. Small groups of them in Boston, New York, and Philadelphia promoted and organized most of the large privately owned transportation and public utility enterprises. They saw the possibilities, and paid the lobbyists needed to secure charters for the major company and for attendant development and construction companies.[26] Their subscriptions to stock and bonds, in either the main company or a construction company, provided a considerable part of the initial funds and gave the banks with which they were connected the confidence to extend loans.

It seems probable that the eastern groups of general entrepreneurs, with their relatively good command of capital and their over-all view of situations, undertook long-range development more rapidly than either institutional or local interests would have. For example, before the Michigan Central reached Chicago the Boston and New York entrepreneurs responsible for its finance were already planning for a western connection; and before the western connection, the Chicago, Burlington & Quincy,

[23] See Chapter IV, above.
[24] See Charlotte Erickson, *American Industry and the European Immigrant, 1860-1885* (Cambridge, Mass.: Harvard University Press, 1957).
[25] Cochran, *The Pabst Brewing Company*, pp. 1 ff.
[26] Thomas C. Cochran, *Railroad Leaders, 1845-1890* (Cambridge: Harvard University Press, 1953), p. 194.

reached the Mississippi the same entrepreneurs were projecting an extension across Iowa.

Entrepreneurs interested in politics, like Stephen A. Douglas, secured a policy of assisting railroads by federal land grants, delivered through the states from 1850 to 1860 and directly from the federal government to projected transcontinental lines from 1862 to 1871. These aided greatly in attracting domestic and foreign capital to railroad construction.[27] Investors who might be skeptical about the immediate earning power of a railroad across the prairies had faith in the ultimate value of the farming land. This seemed particularly true of foreign investors. The land grants undoubtedly drew otherwise unavailable money from England and Continental Europe into projects like the Illinois Central and the Northern Pacific.[28]

State and local credit also played a major part in starting the canal and railroad transportation system. With considerable oversimplification, one might distinguish two stages in the development of both finance and transportation: a first stage in which financially weak entrepreneurs sought the aid of the state and local governments and welcomed state-owned enterprise—as a needed supplement; and a second stage in which stronger general entrepreneurs bought out the government-owned enterprises, retired government-owned securities, and proceeded on a private enterprise basis. The dividing line between these stages depended largely upon the sums required by the projected enterprises in relation to the local supply of capital and the probability of immediate returns. In the East there were few new state activities after 1850, although local subscription to stocks and bonds continued into the 1870's.[29] In the Mississippi Valley state enterprise continued through the 1850's and farther west, state and federal aid was common until the panic of 1873.

[27] Thomas C. Cochran, "Land Grants and Railroad Entrepreneurship," *The Journal of Economic History,* Supplement X, 1950, p. 62.

[28] See Paul W. Gates, *The Illinois Central Railroad and Its Colonization Work* (Cambridge, Mass.: Harvard University Press, 1934); and James B. Hedges, *Henry Villard and the Railways of the Northwest* (New Haven, Ct.; Yale University Press, 1930).

[29] See Pierce, *Railroads of New York,* Chap. I.

Aside from various types of building construction, the greatest demands for capital between 1850 and 1890 came in connection with railroad construction. According to the admittedly inaccurate capital estimates of the federal census there was $533 million invested in manufacturing (including hand and neighborhood industries) in 1849 and only $318 million in railroads. By 1889 the two sums were $6,525 million in manufacturing and $9,680 million in railroads. Henry Adams said, "My generation was mortgaged to the railroads and nobody knew it better than that generation itself."[30] Negotiating and servicing this mortgage constituted the greatest achievement of nineteenth century American entrepreneurs in the field of capital formation.

The feat of assembling nearly $10 billion in capital, largely through the security markets, should not obscure the fact that some of this capital and much of the $6.5 billion credited to manufacturing were the result of reinvested earnings. In industry, marketing, and agriculture, entrepreneurs created capital through successful management that brought in large earnings, coupled with low salary levels and small allocations to dividends or paid-out profits. During the first twenty years of the corporate history of the Pabst Brewing Co., for example, over 75 per cent of net earnings was reinvested and less than 25 per cent paid out in dividends. Up to 1889 the president and vice-president of this company, which was by then worth $5,000,000, drew salaries of $2,500 a year.[31] Other studies in company history indicate that this picture is probably representative of family and other closely owned companies.

IV

So far the emphasis has been on the promoters and managers of enterprise, but the supply of capital for internal improvements was also a function of entrepreneurship in the field of banking,

[30] Henry Adams, *The Education of Henry Adams* (Boston: Houghton Mifflin, 1930), p. 240.
[31] Cochran, *The Pabst Brewing Company*, as cited, pp. 84 and 94.

a product of manipulation and innovation in the mechanics of money and credit. Between 1800 and 1850, American financial entrepreneurs developed institutions to encourage saving and to collect such funds in usable pools.[32] Chartered commercial banks, which had first appeared in 1780, spread rapidly during this period, and savings banks, building and loan associations, and life insurance companies were started. While most of the investment from the latter three types of pooled savings was in urban mortgages, this in turn released other credit for manufacturing and transportation investment.[33]

Laws against branch banking in many states, and the willingness of state legislatures after 1815 to charter banks, led to a great spread of small banking units run on an experimental basis by local entrepreneurs. In 1840 there were 900 banks; by 1861 the number reached 1,600. While there were various state stipulations regarding reserves, taken as a whole the system was capable of expanding credit both rapidly and unwisely. The unwise advances, in turn, led to bank failures and the temporary prostration of local business. Whether a few large banks with branches, such as existed in most European nations, would have produced a more rapid economic growth can probably never be decided. These thousands of banking entrepreneurs lacked expert skill in assessing risks and were therefore likely to be bound by custom in extending credit, but they were close to the needs of their local communities, and they were no doubt influenced by the risk-taking spirit of the local businessmen.

The other major development of this period was the beginning of specialized investment banking. In the early nineteenth century the American agencies for selling securities were numerous and unspecialized. Securities might be contracted or negotiated for by incorporated commercial banks, private banks, general entrepreneurs, foreign bankers or their agents, brokers, or traveling salesmen. Most of these middlemen hoped to sell all or

[32] Redlich, *Moulding of American Banking,* vol. I. See also Ralph W. Hidy, *The House of Baring in American Trade and Finance* (Cambridge: Harvard University Press, 1949) ; and Jenks, *Migration of British Capital.*

[33] Roy A. Foulke, *Sinews of American Commerce* (New York: Dun & Bradstreet, 1941), pp. 89-150.

a large part of the securities abroad. The close connections between American and British financial markets gave investment
in the United States a different aspect from the buying of securities in other underdeveloped areas. The chief British houses,
such as Baring Brothers, Thomas Wilson, or the Rothschilds,
had either trusted correspondents or agents in this country.
Englishmen were used to appraising American commercial risks
and readily shifted to appraising the risks of publicly or privately
financed transportation.

The good standing of American state securities in the British
market, prior to the defaults of 1841, was one reason for the
extensive use of state credit for financing banking and transportation to a total of $224 million.[34] From the late 1940's on,
London provided a fair market for issues of the larger American railroads, while the standing of state securities was still
depressed by defaults. As a result, well-sponsored railroads found
their own bonds more salable than those of most of the states.

But the foreign market was not available to small transportation companies and public utilities or to American manufacturing enterprises. Local money-raisers resorted to many devices.
Lotteries, improvement banks, building and loan companies, and
mortgage banks all appeared within the first two decades of
the nineteenth century. Some of these, such as western improvement or mortgage banks, were schemes for monetizing debt and
then gradually passing the obligations eastward. Underlying
this ingeniousness in creating credit were a faith in the immediate profitability of applying capital to many processes and a
confidence in the general devotion to the goal of money-making.

Throughout the period before the Civil War, commercial
banks were both buyers and middlemen in the investment security business. The Bank of the United States of Pennsylvania,
during its brief career following the end of the federal charter
in 1836, took a leading part in security negotiations. The companies chartered under various state "free banking" acts also
participated in investment business, particularly in state and
municipal securities.

[34] Redlich, *Moulding of American Banking,* I, p. 344.

With the rapid spread of railroads and gas and water companies, private bankers found their investment business becoming more important in relation to the old stand-bys of note brokerage and foreign and domestic exchange. August Belmont, as American agent for the Rothschilds; Prime Ward & King; George Peabody; Drexel; Brown Brothers; E. W. Clark; Corcoran & Riggs; and Vermilye were among the houses that became sufficiently specialized to be called investment bankers in the years before the Civil War.

The federal flotations of $2.5 billion in public debt during the Civil War resulted in an expansion of American financial markets. The handling of the contracting, selling, and refunding of these issues added to the strength of a few specialized houses that, with the exception of Jay Cooke & Co., were to dominate the security markets in the United States for the next sixty years. In the post-Civil War period, as in earlier years, the strength of houses such as Drexel-Morgan, J. & W. Seligman, or Kidder, Peabody lay largely in good foreign connections, while the fatal weakness of Jay Cooke was his failure to establish real strength in London, Paris, Amsterdam, Berlin, or Frankfurt.

Between 1865 and 1880, American investment banking entrepreneurs developed the underwriting and selling syndicate and the practices of banker leadership and responsibility in the affairs of their major clients. It is hard to estimate the effect of these practices on capital formation. Cooperation in selling syndicates probably mobilized more of the nation's savings for large-scale projects than might have been reached through the earlier, less highly organized efforts, but research would be needed to demonstrate this.

Still harder to judge is the effect of banker leadership, as illustrated by J. Pierpont Morgan. From the late 1870's on, Morgan asked for and received representation on the boards of certain railroads that he financed; by the middle 1880's he insisted on companies retaining the services of the syndicate leaders responsible for outstanding issues, at least in the case of his own clients;[35] and by the 1890's he was initiating reorganizations and mergers of railroads and industrial companies. Morgan's efforts probably drew more foreign capital into the United States than would have come otherwise, but the effect of his plans was often to check the rate of expansion of a road or an industry so that new commitments would not endanger the servicing of senior securities. Other leaders in the investment banking field operated in much the same fashion. These bankers also tended to share the view that monopoly created stability and a well-ordered economy, whereas competition was upsetting and dangerous.

V

While nineteenth century American culture appears to have been one of the most favorable in world history for entrepreneurial activity, there were certain negative elements stemming either from the general environment or from the attitude of certain groups of entrepreneurs. Insofar as these elements curtailed or reduced the vigor of creative entrepreneurial activity, they may be assumed to have hindered capital formation.

One type of hindrance to effective entrepreneurial action was maladjustment between labor supply and demand. With the shifting of industry resulting from technological change, adjustment in the case of labor presumably never approaches close to perfection, but the process of internal westward growth and European immigration to the eastern seaboard imposed unusual difficulties on the United States.[36] The decline of agricultural activities after about 1830 in parts of the Northeast and an already large population tended to produce a regional surplus of native-born labor. From the 1840's on, immigrants arrived in the eastern ports at a rate generally in excess of the growth of opportunities for local employment. How to draw effectively

---

[35] Cochran, *Railroad Leaders*, p. 71.
[36] See H. J. Habakkuk, *American and British Technology in the Nineteenth Century* (Cambridge, Eng.: Cambridge University Press, 1962).

upon these pools of labor was an entrepreneurial challenge throughout the last half of the nineteenth century. Business-men tried a number of expedients. Associations were formed in the 1850's to move labor westward, chiefly at the expense of employers interested in western ventures. The difficulty with this device was lack of any guarantee that the laborer would arrive and work satisfactorily to repay the cost of his trans-portation. Some samples of the numbers actually moved make it appear that most entrepreneurs regarded the risk as too great. Railroads made arrangements to move workers westward for their own purposes, often with land as an ultimate reward for fulfillment of the labor contract. Western states and territories, anxious to gain population, established eastern and European agencies to encourage migration. From the Civil War on, some companies made a business of importing Asiatic or European workers under contract, but the practice was prohibited by acts of Congress in 1882 and 1885, respectively. The extent to which these devices equated supply and demand has still to be investigated.

A second set of possible retarding factors stemmed from sec-tional and local rivalries and ambitions that led entrepreneurs or their political representatives to sacrifice the general to what seemed the special welfare. Part of the division of opinion came from geographical position, and part from differing types of entrepreneurship. The large export agriculturist thought in terms, and had real economic interests, different from those of the protected small manufacturer. Geographical-occupational cleavages led not only to conflicts over national policy, but also to a rather general preference for locally instead of centrally controlled activities. Sometimes Congress was swayed by local interests from all parts of the nation, as in state banker opposi-tion to central banking; at other times the interest represented might be more strictly sectional, as illustrated in the New England fear of loss of labor as a result of more liberal land laws.

Here again the effects of these pressures on capital formation have never been determined. Although central banking, for example, would have given businessmen a uniform currency and solved some domestic exchange problems, it would also have tended to curtail credit inflation, which was one of the important factors in capital formation during the sharp upswings of the business cycle. It is hard to tell whether the entrepreneurial pressure that contributed to the writing of federal land laws in 1785 and 1796, under which very little land was sold, had any considerable effect on the westward movement, since the surrounding states had ample land for sale on favorable terms. If the laws did check migration, it is also hard to tell what effect this had on economic growth.[37] The eastern business argument that labor was needed there for commerce and industry and that western investment under existing conditions of transportation was lost to the national economy undoubtedly had some truth.

The planter-entrepreneurs who represented the slave plantation system in Washington on many occasions blocked policies that might have aided industrial capital formation. The most obvious issue involved was the protective tariff. Except in 1816, the South was opposed to protection, and, aided by northern railroad and commercial interests, it managed to prevent or modify tariff increases prior to 1861. The probable effect on the United States of a high rather than the moderate tariff policy prior to the Civil War is a question that has occupied economic thinkers for more than a century without a conclusive answer being produced.

The planters came to fear the social effect of creating an urban Negro working population, and, after a brief period of encouragement to local industry from 1815 on, southern investors put their capital to other use, often outside their own region. There has not been sufficient study of southern investment to tell how much of the planters' savings went abroad.

The South, to some extent, had cultural patterns common in underdeveloped agricultural regions in the twentieth century. There was high concentration of income at the top, a general

---

[37] For discussion of the land laws see Arthur C. Bining and Thomas C. Cochran, *The Rise of American Economic Life* (New York: Charles Scribner's, 1963), pp. 153 ff.

estimate for 1860 being that three-quarters of the export income was distributed to about 8,000 families. But in spite of concentration of income, luxurious living standards seemed to prevent the planter elite from promoting a high rate of capital growth.

The problem of the internal efficiency of the specialized slave plantation system is too complex to discuss here.[38] But there is at least a possibility that the planter-entrepreneurs, with their semi-feudal cultural values, stood in the way of more rapid capital growth both in their own section and in the nation as a whole.

The southern influence in Washington was hostile to many policies of the entrepreneurs interested in developing the West. Not only did the westward movement draw population away from the old South, but the slave system could not readily be transplanted to many new territories. While it had been noted that eastern businessmen also were doubtful of the value to them of rapid western growth, after the middle 1840's the combination of heavy immigration and increasing western investment opportunities won many of them over to an expansionist policy. Hence, by the 1850's it was chiefly southern influence that blocked federal subsidies for a centrally located transcontinental railroad, freer disposal of western land, river and harbor development, and other internal improvements. Whether more lavish federal aid in the West at an earlier period would in the long run have contributed to capital growth remains a moot point.

A deterrent to capital investment similar to the rivalry of sectional entrepreneurs in national politics was the power of local or special interests in state legislatures. Businessmen and other citizens of the counties that benefited from the Erie Canal system in New York State, for example, were able up until 1851 to get the legislature to place clauses in railroad charters either

[38] See Emory Q. Hawk, *Economic History of the South* (New York: Prentice-Hall, 1934), pp. 271-273; John S. Spratt, "The Cotton Miner," *American Quarterly*, Fall 1952, pp. 214-235; and John R. Myer and Alfred H. Conrad, "Economic Theory, Statistical Inference, and Economic History," *"The Journal of Economic History*, XVII, 1957, pp. 524-553.

prohibiting the carriage of freight or forcing the payment of canal tolls on railroad shipments.[39] The Camden & Amboy Railroad in New Jersey was able through special charter provisions and political influence to prevent for thirty years the chartering of any competing New York-Philadelphia line.[40] Yet, against all these possible deterrents to capital growth must be set the stimulating effect of reliable, stable government.

A third type of deterrent to entrepreneurial activity and capital growth was the depression phase of business cycles. Fluctuations in prices, business activity, and employment seem to have been more severe than in the nations of Western Europe. As already illustrated, American entrepreneurs appear to have reached greater heights of incautious optimism during booms than did their European counterparts, and consequently the ensuing debacles were more prostrating. On the one hand, the price inflations that usually accompanied upswings undoubtedly led to diminished consumption by receivers of fixed incomes and larger entrepreneurial profits, both of which stimulated capital investment. But the relatively prolonged stagnation in new investment during the major depressions may have offset the extra capital gains of the boom.

Many leading entrepreneurs and some economic writers were aware of a general cyclical movement and understood the merits of countercyclical investment. But to raise capital by security flotation in a depression was extremely difficult. This is abundantly illustrated in the letters of nineteenth century railroad presidents. Even the minor recession of 1848 led John Murray Forbes to write, "At this moment it is impossible to get subscriptions to any Rail Road however promising." Ten years later he counselled, "We [should] let our Stockholders recover from the depression of the past year and regain confidence before we plunge into anything however good." In 1874 John W. Brooks wrote, "The bare idea, even of discussing a new project, would injure one's reputation for sanity." And looking back

[39] Frank W. Stevens, *The Beginnings of the New York Central Railroad* (New York: G. P. Putnam's, 1926), pp. 267-273.

[40] John W. Cadman, Jr., *The Corporation in New Jersey* (Cambridge: Harvard University Press, 1949), pp. 54-59.

on these years, Frederick W. Kimball noted that "During the recent depression nobody would even listen to the establishment of a new enterprise."[41]

A fourth set of deterrents to entrepreneurial action might be put under the heading of insufficient security. This had many forms. The most routine commercial transactions involved risks when conducted across state lines and at a distance. Prior to the spread of the railroad, inland transportation and transfer agents were unreliable. To be sure of receiving goods intact and on time, the inland merchants had to travel with them.[42] Before the beginning of credit agencies in the 1830's, it was difficult to know who could be trusted in distant cities, and unfamiliar bank notes might prove to be depreciated or counterfeit. State courts could impede collection of debts by "foreigners" and the status of corporations doing business outside the state of their incorporation was questionable prior to the 1880's. While the United States was nominally one country, the difficulties of doing some kinds of interstate business in the first half of the nineteenth century were almost as great as though the boundary lines were those of independent nations.

Added to these insecurities arising from poor trade facilities and discriminatory local statutes was a lack of the police protection necessary for maintaining orderly markets. Robbery by stealth or violence was frequent, particularly in the newer regions. Only a few cities had an organized police force.

The low business ethics of many American entrepreneurs were a hindrance both to business efficiency and to the raising of capital. Confidence men selling shares or lots were abundant. Bankruptcy with concealed assets was a common recourse for avoiding embarrassing obligations. Capital was frequently squandered in ways that made it hard to draw the line between overoptimism and outright dishonesty. In building the western railroads, for example, construction was often managed and partly financed by local entrepreneurs who were, at the least, somewhat careless in handling easterners' money. But corporate

---

[41] Quoted in Cochran, *Railroad Leaders,* pp. 105, 106.
[42] See Atherton, *The Pioneer Merchant in Mid-America.*

stockholders were also defrauded by eastern operators of apparently high standing. Railroads were gutted by construction companies controlled by the railroad officers. Presidents of corporations printed fake stock certificates and sold them on the exchanges. Contracts were freely broken when it was inconvenient to live up to them. A result of such entrepreneurial practices was unquestionably to discourage investment in the common stock of corporations.

A related deterrent to investment in stock was the lack of regulation of security exchanges and original prospectuses. Let the buyer beware was completely the rule up until the late 1860's. Then after Drew, Fisk, and Gould had swindled Commodore Vanderbilt by wholesale printing of stock certificates, the New York Stock Exchange regulated itself to the extent of demanding information on the total number of shares issued by a company whose stock was traded on the Exchange. But the states and the federal government continued their laissez-faire attitude. The effect was to increase the preference of the conservative investor for mortgages or for forms of local equities where he could keep watch on the entrepreneurs who had his money.

VI

By the end of the nineteenth century the rate of net capital formation was declining slightly in comparison with the rate of increase in either national income or gross national product, and the latter two series in turn were advancing at a less rapid rate than in earlier decades. The apparent turn of the curve was undoubtedly affected by changing cultural factors that have not been subjected to analysis sufficient to support generalizations. The effect of the West as a promised land and a stimulant to saving and investment was probably lessening. The problems of urban industrial society were emphasizing security and de-emphasizing individual initiative, risk-taking and the "puritan" attitude. The confidence that change meant progress was probably less than in earlier years. A doctrine of consumption was threatening the doctrine of frugality and thrift. But in addition to these and similar deterrents to capital formation, the changing character of entrepreneurship played a part.

A number of important changes in the entrepreneurial situation were unfavorable to capital formation: the increase in the size of companies, with an attendant bureaucratization of entrepreneurial functions; the substitution of professional executives for owner-managers; the greater persistence of monopolies and other large organizations regardless of economic efficiency; the inheritance of managerial functions by less able heirs; the supersedure of the influence of general entrepreneurs by that of investment banking houses and other financial institutions; and the deterring effect of taxes and government regulation.

In the large companies that appeared rapidly beginning in the 1880's, the chief executives frequently rose through the ranks. They succeeded by being "good organization men" with a proper regard for loyalties and morale. A study by Mabel Newcomer of the careers of the top executives of the largest nonfinancial corporations for 1899, 1923, and 1948 shows the increasing trend away from independent business backgrounds. Including in her "entrepreneur-capitalist" group (those who have run their own business) "bankers, brokers, and those engineers and lawyers who had a hand in organizing the corporation which they head," she finds that three-fifths of the 1899 group fall in this category, one-third of the 1923 group, and only one-quarter of the 1948 group.[43] The attitude of professional entrepreneurs toward liquidation or serious risk-taking was likely, to say the least, to be more conservative than that of the owner-manager or the general entrepreneur.

Not only was the salaried professional disinclined to pursue policies that might eliminate his job, regardless of the profitability of these policies to the stockholders, but he might also be loath to recommend investments that would upset personal

---

[43] "The Chief Executive of Large Business Corporations," *Explorations in Entrepreneurial History*, October 1952, pp. 13-14. See also the articles by Winifred Gregory and Irene Neu and by William Miller in *Men in Business*.

relations within the organization. For example, the assets of a steamship company became almost completely liquid during World War II through the sinking of its vessels and resulting insurance payments. There was little prospect that the company's normal trade would be profitable for new vessels in time of peace. The chairman of the board, a large stockholder, and independent capitalist played with the idea of liquidating the operating end of the business and investing the capital in more promising enterprises. Profit considerations pointed overwhelmingly in that direction. But none of the professional managers in the company, whose jobs would disappear, favored such a plan. In the end the company decided to continue its customary type of operations. The pressures of personal relations and the momentum of a going concern won out over what appeared to promise maximization of profit for the stockholders.

These considerations plus that of size alone, and threatened government prosecution under the antitrust laws, tended to make big-company entrepreneurs think more in terms of maintaining a given market position and stabilizing sales than in terms of continued technological innovation and expansion at the expense of competitors. Furthermore, if one or a limited number of companies controlled production in an industry, it was possible for entrepreneurs to slow down the pace of innovation in the interest of reducing risk and lengthening the period of utilization of existing equipment—a process that might increase immediate purchasing power but slow down capital formation and future production. Well-known illustrations of the slowing down of innovation in the interests of more complete utilization of existing equipment are the American Telephone & Telegraph's treatment of the hand-set phone after 1907, and General Electric's and Westinghouse's relatively slow response to the possibilities of fluorescent lighting between 1896 and 1938.[44]

[44] See N. R. Danielian, *A. T. & T.* (New York: Vanguard Press, 1939). pp. 102-103, and Arthur A. Bright, Jr., *The Electric-Lamp* (New York: The Macmillan Co., 1949), pp. 384-391. Paul G. Clark in *The Structure of American Economy, 1919-1939* (Wassily Leontief, ed., 2nd ed., 1951; New York: Oxford University Press), pictures the investment policy of A. T. & T. as a kind of automatic adjustment to demand on a basis worked out by engineers. Entrepreneurial decisions do not appear explicitly.

If complete figures could be assembled, it might turn out that, other things being equal, the larger a firm the longer its life expectancy. Sampling studies point in this direction. But if the longevity is because of size rather than economic efficiency, the prolongation of the large unit presumably hinders new capital investment and ultimately retards the increase of productivity in the industry. Looked at from the standpoint of the present discussion, this is another example of diminished entrepreneurial efficiency in capital allocation resulting from bigness.

There have been no quantitative studies of the qualitatively recognized shift in entrepreneurship from the founding generations in medium and big business to the sons and heirs of the founders. The period 1880 to 1910 would appear to embrace many such shifts. It seems likely, from isolated case studies, that the second generation tended to be both less able and less interested in expansion than its predecessor.[45]

During the same period the increasing size of security flotations, the better organization of the American money market, and the rise of strong American investment banks and insurance and trust companies all deprived the general entrepreneur of his control over capital and thereby weakened his authority. The bankers institutionalized general entrepreneurial functions, and the representatives of banking houses took the independent financier's place of authority on boards of directors. The effect seems to have some similarity to that of the replacement of owner-managers by professionals. The investment bankers were interested in stability and "sound" financial practices which would tend to insure the servicing of bonds. They were often unwilling to agree to new investments requiring security issues unless these fitted in with the anticipated movements of the stock market or their general financial plans.

Some new industries, when they reached the point of needing large capital issues, were held back by the conservatism of insti-

[45] A number of business histories illustrate this point. Among them see Harold F. Williamson, *Winchester* (Combat Forces Press, 1952); C. W. Moore, *Timing a Century* (Cambridge: Harvard University Press, 1945); Thomas Navin, *The Whitin Machine Works since 1831* (Cambridge: Harvard University Press, 1950); and Cochran, *The Pabst Brewing Company*.

tutionalized financial entrepreneurship. The automobile and moving picture industries offer illustrations. In automobiles, investment bankers refused to back W. C. Durant's original organization of General Motors. When this company finally secured banker aid in 1910 the conditions were onerous financially and involved effective banker control of the company during the lifetime of the loan. Under this system, for the next five years, General Motors sales increased less rapidly than those of the industry as a whole.[46] In motion pictures Fox and Loew both encountered Wall Street indifference or hostility. In other words, the bankers represented conservative elements generally opposed to taking new types of risk, even though the latter might promise considerable economic gain if successful.

The deterring effect of tax and regulatory policies on entrepreneurial capital formation has been written about extensively. For instance, the relative failure of the railroads to improve their capital structure and equipment between 1910 and 1918 is blamed by competent scholars on the psychologically discouraging effect of overzealous regulation by the Interstate Commerce Commission. The failure to achieve satisfactory net private capital formation during the 1930's has frequently been blamed on the effect of New Deal regulations on entrepreneurial initiative.

The diversion of capital into enterprises lacking comparative advantage by tariffs and subsidies is another example of government "interference." Entrepreneurs would not have invested in new American merchants ships from 1936 on, save for large-scale government subsidy. Insofar as the economy had unemployed resources in this period, such allocation of capital may have cost nothing, but in principle it produced facilities available more cheaply from foreign nations.

It seems likely that the direct effect of regulation is always adverse to entrepreneurial initiative, but rate-fixing, for example, may have an indirectly stimulating effect on technological innovation. An ex-president of a telephone company remarked

[46] Ralph Epstein, *The Automobile Industry* (Chicago: A. W. Shaw, 1928), p. 221.

in conversation that A. T. & T. had to depend on research and resulting improvements in order to make the profits necessary for dividends and expansion under a system of government-controlled rates.

Against this list of possible deterrents to active and intelligent entrepreneurial risk-taking arising from twentieth century conditions should be set some favorable factors: increasing public willingness to invest in stock exchange securities; the accumulation of large pools of small savings by banks and insurance companies; the employment of specialists, such as industrial engineers, economists, and accountants, who, aided by business periodicals and special reports, tended to produce more calculated and presumably more efficient investment policies; the persistence of small business; sharply rising expenditures for research from World War II on; and direct government aids to, and tax incentives for, investment.

Increasing public familiarity with security investment arose from many sources. Urban middle and upper class income-receivers were getting a larger percentage of the total income as urban population became larger in relation to rural, and as entrepreneurial, managerial, and professional occupations increased. This group was, presumably, more likely to invest in securities than was the farm or small-town population. As business units grew larger, more were publicly financed and the securities of old, well-established companies offered reasonably safe investment. In addition, increasingly active security-selling by banks and brokerage houses from 1897 to 1929 and the government bond-selling campaigns of World War I added to the ranks of security-holders. Hence, entrepreneurs could undertake large ventures with more assurance of adequate and economical financing.

In this connection it may be noted that as successful companies came to provide more of their working capital from profits or security issues, the demand for short-term renewable loans began to fall, particularly in the major metropolitan areas. As a result, banker-entrepreneurs in the 1920's were forced to do more of their lending with securities as collateral, and to buy more securities for bank portfolios than in previous decades. This transferred much of the strain of the 1929-1933 decline from other enterprises to the banks themselves. Whereas short-term loans had in general been collectable, the banks were now left holding securities that in some cases declined to a fraction of their former value. However, the problems of banker entrepreneurship in the 1920's and 1930's have been so thoroughly discussed and investigated that nothing can be added here.

The accumulation of vast capital pools from insurance policy premiums and bank deposits went on rapidly from the 1890's, partly as a result of aggressive selling campaigns by insurance and banking entrepreneurs. The life insurance companies granted large areas to central agents, to be exploited on a commission basis. Banks fought for deposits by sending salesmen to call on the more substantial businessmen and by advertising extensively to attract small depositors.[47] Investment trusts also drew the savings of small investors into large pools. After World War II, pension funds became an important form of pooled savings, amounting by 1960 to over $4 billion a year.[48] In addition, corporate savings in the form of reserves against depreciation or depletion represented large blocks of capital available for investment.

Looked at broadly, the increasing emphasis on both personal and corporate financial security was putting the disposition of a large portion of savings into the hands of professional entrepreneurs. Unquestionably, these pooled resources offered an increasingly good market for securities regarded as safe investments. Between 1947 and 1951 about 40 per cent by value of

[47] For insurance see Shepard B. Clough, *A Century of American Life Insurance* (New York: Columbia University Press, 1946), pp. 158-172 and pp. 239-243; Marquis James, *The Metropolitan Life* (New York: The Viking Press, 1947), pp. 340-345; and Owen J. Stalson, *Marketing Life Insurance* (Cambridge: Harvard University Press, 1942), pp. 508-658. There is no adequate history of the entrepreneurial and marketing aspects of banking in the twentieth century.

[48] For more on these new forms of savings and investment see Donald L. Kemmerer, "The Marketing of Securities, 1930-1952," *The Journal of Economic History*, Fall 1952, pp. 454-468.

the new security issues were sold privately to other companies. In the case of large corporate issuers and large buyers, investment bankers had no entrepreneurial role in the proceedings. But the bankers could still put small issuers in touch with small insurance companies and collect a "finder's fee."

The entrepreneurs of commercial banks and insurance companies also took a direct part in allocating capital for long-run uses through term loans. To improve their languishing businesses in the middle 1930's, banks started lending funds to selected customers on a periodic amortization basis for as long as ten years. After World War II, bank terms were generally cut to five years, but insurance companies were often prepared to assume such a loan for ten years more. Through amendment of state laws, life insurance companies and trustees were permitted to invest limited amounts in equities. In this way insurance executives in the 1930's became entrepreneurs of housing development. At this same time the taking over of collateral forced banker-entrepreneurs, temporarily at least, into equity ownership.

As with most of the twentieth century changes discussed here, the effect of this minor revolution in financial practices on net capital formation seems ambiguous. A much larger proportion of total savings than ever before was automatically mobilized and put in the hands of entrepreneurs. Or conversely, the private investor had relatively less to say about the formation of capital. But the professional entrepreneurs who control the funds have to view them in general as reserves whose value must be protected rather than as capital that can properly be put into high-risk, high-profit enterprises. On this basis small businessmen claim to be largely prevented from drawing upon these corporate funds, while the local man of large income, with his savings cut by insurance, pensions, and taxes, cannot perform his historical role of risk-taking investor.

The spread of business information firms, expert consultants, and other special services, leading presumably to what Arthur H. Cole has called a more cognitive type of entrepreneurship, went on rapidly around the turn of the century. Companies set up legal departments, authorized shop procedure analyses, introduced cost accounting, and made more use of forecasting. Insofar as these expedients increased the efficiency of production, they added to the value of already-invested capital, and thereby increased total capital. But the battle was far from one-sided. As studies of the relative efficiency of large and medium-sized businesses have indicated, some of these special services, at least, scarcely compensate for the problems in forecasting and operation introduced by the increasing size of companies.

Over the last 150 years management has been hard pressed to keep pace with the changes introduced by new technology. It does not seem a foregone conclusion that the large-company entrepreneur of today, with a high percentage of specialized staff among his employees, is necessarily better able to cope with his particular environment than was the owner-manager of the early nineteenth century selling in local or regional markets. It is possible that the "revolution in transportation" and the rapid growth of a competitive national market outdistanced the devices of management in the mid-nineteenth century and produced a period of relatively poorly informed entrepreneurship for which this later flowering of special services offered a cure.[49]

The rise of large bureaucratic organizations in which decisions were made by professional administrators should not obscure the fact that a large part of the capital allocation in the economy has remained in the hands of small enterprisers. According to both the Commerce Department and Dun & Bradstreet's listings of firms, the number of enterprises has somewhat more than kept pace with United States population increase during the twentieth century.[50] Including the policy-making officials of large companies, therefore, the percentage of Americans engaged in entrepreneurial activity other than agriculture has substantially increased. Many of these smaller firms, to be sure,

[49] For criticism of the general inefficiency of iron and steel entrepreneurs in the 1870's see Andrew Carnegie, *Autobiography* (New York: Doubleday, 1923), pp. 129 ff.

[50] Rudolph Jones, *The Relative Position of Small Business in the American Economy* (Washington: Catholic University of America Press, 1952) , pp. 34-35.

are not in a position to seek more of the market by reducing prices, although almost any of them may grow by offering better service. Many operate in specialized markets that do not encourage expansion through additional capital investment in that particular business. But in general it may be assumed that in this small-industry, -transportation, and -service area of the economy, many of the entrepreneurial culture patterns of the nineteenth century still persist.

There are also substantial regions of the United States that still are underdeveloped areas. Large parts of the South and Southwest have lacked the managerial and labor skills necessary to establish a broad pattern of industrialization. In West Texas, for example, as late as 1950 entrepreneurs interested in investing in new types of industry often found the banks ready to finance only cattle, oil, crops, and a few other old lines of activity.[51] Furthermore, the federal tax law allowing a large deduction for depletion encourages further investment in oil, and the price support program reinforces cultural leanings toward investment in agricultural land.

Therefore, while it may be affirmed that these underdeveloped areas foster a relatively high degree of entrepreneurial energy in capital allocation, this is often expressed in specialized and limited ways. Both the Texas and southern California bankers and businessmen interviewed in 1950 presumed that the general level of assessment of industrial risk and wise allocation of capital were highest in the old centers of the East and Middle West.

For these reasons, and because of the high stage of development of big companies in the older industrial areas, much of the new development of the resources of the Gulf Coast, the Rocky Mountain states, and even the Pacific Coast is being carried on by branches of established national concerns.

While in certain lines of business the entrepreneur may have his range of choice curtailed by bureaucratic or monopolistic arrangements, government has provided him with increasing

[51] Thomas C. Cochran, *The American Business System* (Cambridge: Harvard University Press, 1957; Harper Torchbook edition, 1962), p. 173.

facilities and safeguards for conducting his operations. Highway and bridge construction in conjunction with the motor vehicle have made major investments possible in new areas and have encouraged entrepreneurs to relocate plants.[52] Improved police and fire protection and more uniform state laws have all encouraged investment in new areas. Only in the twentieth century have some parts of the United States become sufficiently regulated to permit the easy conduct of business. There has been too little historical study of twentieth century business, and of the service group in particular, to estimate the stimulating effect of these factors on entrepreneurship.

Finally, the allocation of capital by entrepreneurs has been profoundly influenced since 1940 by government military policy. Entrepreneurs have been partially relieved of the necessity of deciding what forms new investment should take. The nineteenth century situation of obvious needs in excess of capital resources has been largely recreated. Under these circumstances it is difficult to estimate the role of the entrepreneur in capital formation under conditions of stabilized government demand and fewer shortages in productive resources.

VII

A survey of the history of American capital formation, which prior to 1940 was directed to a large extent by the imagination of entrepreneurs, supports the hypothesis that growth depended more on where and how capital was invested than on the absolute quantity of voluntary savings. Well-managed capital increased rapidly from the reinvestment of earnings. In good times entrepreneurs, largely through the mechanisms of banking, drew on credit in excess of savings—in fact, without much regard for the immediate level of domestic saving. Resulting inflations forced involuntary saving on those receiving fixed incomes.

A very large part of the capital goods created by these entre-

[52] See K. William Kapp, *The Social Costs of Private Enterprise* (Cambridge: Harvard University Press, 1950).

preneurs had ultimate economic value, even though the original promoters may have failed to produce early profits. Capital invested in transportation paid enormous economic returns through the opening up of natural resources, which included coal in close proximity to iron ore. Similarly, investment in manufacturing brought ultimate profits because of cheap fuel and raw materials and the large home market made available by transportation. But if the resources in agricultural land or minerals had been less, the same quantity of initial capital and the same diligence in operation would not have produced the same end results or given the same incentives to further effort. Entrepreneurial activity is seen, therefore, as related to the easy availability of resources, to an initially low man-land ratio, a rapid increase in population, and the security afforded by stable government.

The precise influence of the entrepreneur in this capital growth is as difficult to measure as is the influence of any single factor mentioned above. Such social complexes cannot be broken down into measurable factors, and must, for the present at least, be treated as *Gestalts*. The whole process of which entrepreneurial energy was a part changed significantly over the period. To men of the nineteenth century brought up in Western European traditions it was obvious that America needed transportation, and that transportation would eventually pay for itself. To say the same thing in general economic terms, there were valuable resources that could be exploited by the existing technology. The cost of railroads or canals over long distances was very high; for sixty years after 1830 there was this major industrial use for capital. Large additional sums were necessary to bring high grade mines into effective production. With abundant materials, simple machines promised good returns from mass production. In this complex, rewards for individual success were high. All that was needed for rapid growth was for entrepreneurial imagination to proceed in the routine patterns of the culture.

The ending of what may very tentatively be called the early or pioneer stage of industrial economy and the rise of large corporate business units changed the character of the complex leading to growth. Judging by Kuznets' figures on the declining rate of net capital formation and by the increasing percentage of non-agricultural businessmen in the population, the change appears, up to 1940 at least, to have retarded activities leading to capital formation by entrepreneurs. The superseding of independent financiers (general entrepreneurs) by investment bankers, the rise of professional, salaried managers, the growing complexity of the industrial economy, and the increase of government taxation and controls all appear to have worked against imaginative risk-taking.

Some leading scholars of the subject have been led to the belief that private entrepreneurship is destroying itself by its own creations of bigness and planning.[53] Whether or not this view is correct, there seems no doubt that the entrepreneur of the mid-twentieth century operates in a different cultural setting and responds to different motivations than did his predecessor of 1850. Meanwhile, the large-scale entrance of the federal government as a user of capital equipment tends to obscure the underlying economic trends in entrepreneurial risk-taking or capital allocation and use. Under these circumstances, with the entrepreneur hemmed in by bureaucracy, complexity, and political action, it is hard to forecast his role in capital formation.

[53] See Joseph A. Schumpeter, *Capitalism, Socialism and Democracy* (New York: Harper & Brothers, 1942; Harper Torchbook edition, 1962), and Fritz Redlich, "The Business Leader as a 'Daimonic' Figure, II," *American Journal of Economics and Sociology*, April 1953, pp. 289-299.

VI: Cultural Factors in
Economic Development*

Obviously, entrepreneurship is a factor dependent on its social setting. Economic theorists bringing their analytical methods to bear on problems of growth also discovered that all of economic development is a cultural process in which it is difficult to segregate the economic factors. As Professors Buchanan and Ellis have said: "the really fundamental problems of economic growth are non-economic," or as Irving Siegel put it: "man's ends are overwhelmingly cultural."[1] The obvious corollary of such conclusions is that economic history and growth theory have to be broadly inclusive social studies.

The beginning of the general application of anthropological and sociological concepts to what was conventionally regarded as the field of economic history came during World War II. Inspired by Arthur H. Cole the Committee on Research in Economic History sponsored conferences that ultimately led to the Center for Research in Entrepreneurial History at Harvard. From this and several other groups came new concentration on man and his culture. The entrepreneurial group, particularly, tended to the view that: "The fundamental problem of development consists in generating and energizing human action in a certain direction."[2]

* Reprinted with permission from *The Journal of Economic History*, XX, 4 (Dec. 1960), pp. 515-530.

[1] Norman S. Buchanan and Howard S. Ellis, *Approaches to Economic Development* (New York: Twentieth Century Fund, 1955), p. 405; Siegel in: Social Science Research Council, *Items*, XIV (June, 1960), p. 14.

[2] Albert O. Hirschman, *The Strategy of Economic Development* (New Haven: Yale University Press, 1958), p. 25.

Obviously the new interests pose the same elusive problems in the integration of economic, social, and psychological knowledge that the historian has always had to face, but agreeing with T. S. Ashton that "it would be unwise to begin with a disquisition on economic theory—for the fruit of that tree often turns out to be an apple of discord."[3] I shall only discuss some findings on the effect of cultural difference on business or entrepreneurial behavior, and suggest possible relations to economic change.

Among historians the necessity of comparative studies has long been a cliché, a need that everyone talked about and no one met. During the last fifteen years, however, economic growth has been one of several interests that have made comparative study a reality. When trying to understand the relations of the wide array of variables present in most real situations, comparison with what has taken place in analogous situations in other times and nations offers special insights. Most of the following discussion is grounded on comparisons and contrasts between United States and Latin American experience. The three Latin countries studied represent different modifications of Spanish culture overseas. Puerto Rico, a Spanish military bastion until 1898, has strong elements of traditional Spanish culture. Argentina represents a blending of an original Spanish background with the cultures of waves of immigrants from other European nations, particularly Italy. Less cosmopolitan than Argentina, Mexico has modified Spanish traditions with indigenous Indian customs. Yet all three share a number of cultural characteristics that differ from those of the United States.[4]

A North American turning to the study of Latin American entrepreneurial behavior is at once impressed by the fact that responses to apparently similar situations are not the same. Many of the variations in response are associated with differ-

[3] Thomas S. Ashton, *Economic Fluctuations in England 1700-1800* (Oxford, Eng.: Oxford University Press, 1959), p. 1.
[4] Together with various associates, I have done research in Argentina and Puerto Rico. For Mexico I am relying on John Fayerweather, *The Executive Overseas* (Syracuse: Syracuse University Press, 1959).

ences in social structure and cultural attitudes. Some of the
latter may, in turn, be products of geographical and economic
conditions, but at a given time they exist as separate forces in
the economic situation. Such factors can be discussed in the
language of social structure, statuses, norms and roles, but, as
shown in the following chapter, this vocabulary requires a good
deal of definition and elaboration. For the broad national differences in entrepreneurship discussed here it is easier to use
the anthropological language of culture and personality.

In this vocabulary the Latin American and the United States
styles can be said to be the result of certain persistent basic
cultural attitudes interrelated with different economic behavior.
If one were to pursue the concept of general cultural attitudes
in detail, it would appear that they are a combination of generally held beliefs acting on the modal personality types of the
culture. For purposes of the present survey it is not necessary
to hypothesize the details of such interconnection. The term
"cultural characteristics" will be used to indicate either the attitudes or the behavior arising from the culture-personality complex.

I propose the general hypothesis that certain characteristics of
Latin American culture have been relatively unfavorable to economic development. If this is true, it follows that diverse rates
of development in the two culture areas are not adequately
explained by differences in the physical situation. There is a
generally uniform difference in human response that will upset
calculations based on short- or long-run theories developed under
the suppositions of any one culture.

By contrast to his counterpart in the United States the Latin
entrepreneur enjoys talk, theory, and speculation, and lacks the
compulsion to act. John Gillin finds Latin American culture
"characterized by logic and dialectics, rather than empiricism
and pragmatics; the word is valued more highly than the thing;
the manipulation of symbols (as in argument) is more cultivated
than the manipulation of natural forces and objects (as in mechanics)."[5] John Fayerweather, on the basis of studies in Mexico,

As quoted in Thomas C. Cochran, *The Puerto Rican Businessman*
(Philadelphia: University of Pennsylvania Press, 1959), p. 127.

calls one form of this addiction to speculation *projectismo*. "It consists essentially," he says, "of constructing plans without much critical analysis and then assuming the plans to be an accomplished fact."[6] Another facet of the tendency to postpone action is acceptance of the leadership of the occasional man who is both *sympatico,* or in tune with his followers, and prepared to act vigorously. While dictators appear less likely in United States culture, it is also less likely that executives will receive the Latin degree of support from their chief subordinates.

The Latin American strives more for status not based on business success. This may be a disappearing vestige of agrarian aristocracy, but in Latin America it remains strong. Artistic achievement, professional status, land ownership, and government or military office still outrank anything short of outstanding business success. In Mexico "the best men go into the professions and those who do not, no matter how good their reasons, are always aware that they are considered inferior."[7] Hence Latin entrepreneurs divert their resources to achieving prominence in more prestigious fields. The leading businessman of Puerto Rico for example, is also a member of the Commonwealth legislature and the leader of the conservative party. One of the most important Argentinian entrepreneurs, a man unusually engrossed in his business, took the time to study for and achieve an engineering degree at the University, subsequently held an associate professorship and developed a large *estancia,* all during the most active years of his business career.[8]

A further aspect of seeking prestige in other terms than money is illustrated by the same Argentinian. Between 1928 and 1930 he organized companies in Brazil, Chile, and Uruguay to manufacture some of the products of the parent firm. All of these ventures lost money, and on the average continued to do so for many years. The losses in 1931 and 1932 put a severe strain upon the whole system, yet all three ventures were kept going.

[6] Fayerweather, *The Executive Overseas,* p. 65.
[7] *Ibid.,* p. 96.
[8] Thomas C. Cochran and Ruben E. Reina, *Entrepreneurship in Argentine Culture* (Philadelphia: University of Pennsylvania Press, 1962), pp. 144-157.

There are strong indications that he suffered these losses for reasons other than anticipation of large returns in the future. Among these reasons were probably the prestige that accrued from being an international businessman, and the head of a family with international interests, in a culture where industrialists were not highly respected.

Child-rearing, education, and family life are the chief processes by which culture and personality are perpetuated with a high degree of stability. According to present ideas of personality development the general characteristics favorable or unfavorable to entrepreneurship and economic growth are largely acquired at this early stage. For example, David C. McClelland argues that "countries where stories told to children have a high 'achievement content' show a higher rate of economic progress."[9] Similarly, as suggested in Chapter I, the traits of cooperation that have produced the "organization man" were probably acquired more from family conditioning and schooling than from an adult environment of large corporate enterprise.

Latin American child-rearing is more family centered, particularly in country areas, than appears to be the case in the United States.[10] "In Mexico," writes Professor Fayerweather, there is a much smaller universe with which one can compete. . . . You don't give a darn about the neighbors. That's another world, but you care intensely whether you have as good a refrigerator as your brother-in-law."[11] Along with the restraints imposed on competitive goals by the tendency to look no further than the family, Professor McClelland thinks that the "solidary" family itself is associated with low achievement motivation.[12] The Latin

[9] David C. McClelland, John W. Atkinson, Russell A. Clark, and Edgar F. Lowell, *The Achievement Motive* (New York: Appleton-Century-Crofts, 1953), p. 329. It is held that "there are limits placed on the development of Achievement by too large discrepancies between expectation and results. . . . If the opportunities are well beyond his capacities, negative affect should result, he may develop an avoidance motive as far as achievement is concerned." p. 65.

[10] David Landy, *Tropical Childhood* (Chapel Hill: University of North Carolina Press, 1959), pp. 238 ff.

[11] Fayerweather, *Executive Overseas*, p. 26.

[12] McClelland, *Achievement Motive*, p. 329.

family conditioning also appears to produce individuals who place more emphasis on the forms of politeness and obedience than on the facts of behavior.[13] This characteristic may appear in later life in the Latin liking for discussion rather than action. In making use of such hypotheses it must be remembered that the middle and upper-middle class Latin American family, the source of most entrepreneurs, has not been adequately studied.[14]

In periods before the use of corporations and holding companies family relationships in all countries have been the cement of the business structure. The operation of the family as an informal social and economic organization of relatives living in the same area was general in the eighteenth century in the older parts of the English colonies and persisted in the later centuries in the east coast agricultural regions. Since people move as a household, not as an extended family group, rapid migration in all newer parts of the United States minimized the influence of the family system.

In Latin America the family system has had a greater strength, a longer persistence, and a more clearly defined structure of authority than existed even in North American regions of out-migration such as the old South. The Latin family recognizes a head (jefe), who is not necessarily the oldest living relative, and he is expected to look out for the family interests. The head, when not the eldest, gets his authority by a sort of implicit democratic process, a recognition of his success and leadership by the members of the family. The head, in turn, particularly in a rich and powerful family, takes his responsibility very seriously. Obligations to the family may readily take preference over the obligations or ethics of business.[15] Rich men wishing to lead carefree, footloose lives may deliberately avoid becoming the head of the family. The superimposing of the family structure on business is a complex process with many ramifications.

[13] Fayerweather, *Executive Overseas*, p. 27.
[14] Cochran, *Puerto Rican Businessman*, p. 121.
[15] Fayerweather, *Executive Overseas*, p. 19.

II

The most intricate and in many ways the most important differences between United States and Latin American culture are in the area conventionally covered by the term individualism. For purposes of a clear analysis it would be well to eliminate this term and talk only of more special cultural traits. But "individualism" has such a firm place in both colloquial and official language that it seems necessary to use it as a category and then define some of its divergent meanings.

If the Latin family system is a way of protecting the individual in his competition with the outside world, Latin individualism can be seen as an inner use of the same devices. A man prides himself on possessing a unique inner quality that is divorced from external matters. Only by long intimacy can this inner uniqueness be appreciated and any premature opening of the "soul" to a friend is degrading. Yet all human contacts are approaches to this ideal understanding, and at an early stage the Latin feels or does not feel a mutual sympathy and reacts accordingly. *Sympatico* may be evident quickly to sensitive Latins and the ultimate success or failure of a negotiation may be established within the first few minutes. Professor Gillin notes, for example, the lack of the type of impersonal confidence that men in the United States place in the salesman of large respected corporations. In Latin America "you have to know him as an individual and to understand his 'soul' really to have confidence in him."[16] The attitude gives rise to the characteristic of *personalismo,* loyalty to one with whom an understanding has been achieved.

In contrast so-called individualism in the United States is characterized by striving for status and success in the eyes of a peer group—to be as good or better than the next man. In other words, an individualism supported by external criteria. "It is not, on the whole," wrote Clyde Kluckhohn, the American's "privilege to develop individual uniqueness, to cultivate individuality."[17]

[16] As quoted in Cochran, *Puerto Rican Businessman,* p. 126.
[17] Richard Hays Williams, ed., *Human Factors in Military Operations:*

Another way of expressing the difference in attitudes is to say that the Latin American has an ego-focused image of a situation, while the North American has a cooperative or group-focused approach. Over-emphasis by social scientists on the creative side of entrepreneurship has obscured the importance of these cooperative qualities. Albert Hirschman, on the basis of his wide Latin American experience, argues that the "ego-focused image of change" is a deterrent to economic development because success is not conceived as the result of systematic work and creative effort by a team or group, "combined perhaps with 'a little bit of luck', but is due either to sheer luck or outwitting others through careful scheming. . . . The ego-oriented approach," continues Hirschman, hinders the ability "to bring and hold together an able staff, to delegate authority, to inspire loyalty, to handle successfully relations with labor and the public and a host of managerial talents."[18] William Schurz, a lifelong observer of Latin customs wrote that the Latin American "is not a good organization man, and his conferences and committees would be the despair of an American chairman."[19]

In contrast to the value placed on objectivity and impersonality among United States businessmen, the Latin American tends to regard seeking inner satisfaction, giving in to his "feelings," as the proper course, one which is taken for granted by people of his culture and needs no apology. This means, in turn, that he may refuse to do business with someone he dislikes, that he follows prearranged plans only in so far as they suit his feelings, and that he may initiate unsound projects, chiefly because they appeal to his emotions. Furthermore, since these characteristics are well understood, the Latin American anticipates them in his fellow businessmen. What might be regarded as a breach of faith in the United States is understood to be a justifiable change in feeling.

Some Application of the Social Sciences to Operations Research (Chevy Chase, Md.: Operations Research Office, The Johns Hopkins University, 1954), pp. 119-20.
[18] Hirschman, *Strategy of Economic Development*, pp. 16-17.
[19] As quoted in Cochran, *Puerto Rican Businessman*, p. 123.

Ego-centric personality is also associated with greater emphasis on personal dignity. *Dignidad,* as the attitude is often called, can be seen as another facet of the devices to protect the ego from competition. The Latin Americans may scheme just as imaginatively for advantage, but they are disinclined to take overt acts which might expose them to humiliation in case of failure. Former Governor Rexford G. Tugwell said that the Puerto Rican "possesses a pride which is almost an obsession and which leads frequently to the substitution of fancy for fact . . . to the avoidance of outside competition, to the protection of mediocrity and so to a general lowering of levels of competence."[20]

Like other people, Latin Americans have always had to take criticism. "Offenses to *dignidad* have been commonplace . . .", but "they cannot take criticism and respond to it as part of a democratic context . . . one side of a democratic process of exchanging views. . . ." For example, "in one apparently well-established relationship, critical pressure on an operating problem unnerved a Mexican executive to the point of making several unwise decisions."[21]

The Latin American relation between the chief and his subordinates reproduces the family pattern of paternalism with its emphasis on formal rather than real obedience. The normal framework for deccision is superordinate-subordinate rather than one of equalitarian interchange of ideas or cooperation. The inferior will not risk the humiliation he might feel if he openly contradicted his superior and was then over-ridden, but orders may in fact be neglected. When the subordinate does act he feels safer from assaults upon his dignity when carrying out specific orders.[22]

Consequently delegation of authority is one of the critical points in registering the difference between Latin American and United States attitudes. Often one must look below the surface of organization charts or routine controls to detect the operation of this cultural difference. In giving orders in the fac-

[20] *Ibid.,* p. 125.
[21] Fayerweather, *Executive Overseas,* pp. 164-165.
[22] *Ibid.,* p. 32.

tory the Latin in lower- or middle-management acts with fully as much authority as his counterpart in the United States, but he is to a greater extent passing on orders from one he looks to as a superior rather than using, and risking, his personal judgment in meeting the situation. Extremes of the United States type of delegation are indicated by the policy in some large companies of leaving the problem of improving poor operating results up to the local manager, or by the statement of the president of a large company that he never made decisions because by the time matters reached his office the decisions had all been made. In many large Latin American companies what the United States manager would call delegation of authority from the chief to the subordinate has never taken place.

For example, in the 1930's one of the largest Argentine manufacturing firms had no officer conferences and no elaborate charts or manuals for managerial procedure. The chief walked through the main plant about twice a week conferring with all levels of subordinates down to the foreman and issuing direct orders. His manner was humble and he showed proper respect for the inner uniqueness of the men who talked with him, but he gave the orders on the basis of his personal judgment.

In 1941, however, the Argentinian entrepreneur decided that his plants, employing nearly four thousand people, might profit from more systematic management. A very large United States firm, one of the principle licensors, was asked to send an expert to Argentina to introduce North American managerial efficiency. The United States company sent a recently retired executive who spent nearly a year in Buenos Aires installing a complete system for management and shop procedures. But when put in operation, the system ran into difficulties. To begin with, it was hard to select the new departmental and divisional heads because under the system of one-man control few of the available men had really exercised their own authority, and hence their executive abilities were unknown. Men were finally fitted into the chart, however, and the plan put in operation. After eight months the expert from the United States reported that "organization functions are being ignored . . . engineers are doing shop work, shop officials are doing engineering work, building construction undertaken without informing Maintenance Department, salesmen giving instructions direct to the shop." "During the war," concluded the chief engineer of the company, "they did not do much about the new system. After the war they started again."[23] But even in 1960, with many plants and over 10,000 employees, the company was still highly centralized, with ultimate decision resting largely in the hands of the successor of the original leader. Many United States ideas had been absorbed, but reshaped to fit the customs of Argentine culture.

That these differences are an effect of the personality-culture complex rather than just current fashions in management is further indicated by the fact that able managers in the United States were urging delegation in the nineteenth century. Charles E. Perkins of the Chicago, Burlington & Quincy Railroad, for example, argued in 1882 for a system of semi-autonomous divisions under general managers who could run them more effectively than if "one management were put over the whole."[24]

Contrasts in the environment in which business takes place in the two areas, a reflection of the cultures, accentuates the underlying differences. Valuable information on business or government policy in Latin America is gained in more indirect ways, such as prolonged luncheon conversations. While to be hurried in the United States is a sign of importance, to appear to be a cultured gentleman with leisure is more prestigious in Latin America. Consequently, Latins may linger over lunch and delay important conferences within their company, or enter into some long time-consuming and apparently non-business discussion ultimately to get useful business information.[25]

[23] Cochran and Reina, *Entrepreneurship in Argentine Culture*, pp. 186-189.

[24] Charles E. Perkins to Thomas Potter, May 22, 1882, as quoted in Thomas C. Cochran, *Railroad Leaders 1845-1890* (Cambridge: Harvard University Press, 1953), p. 86.

[25] Much of the time of the entrepreneur studied in Argentina was used in cementing important friendships. See also Fayerweather, *Executive Overseas*, p. 70.

The person wishing to argue against the differentiating effect of cultural elements on economic growth could match the examples used with ones from the United States. North American entrepreneurs have taken uneconomic actions because of personal antagonisms, embarked on poorly planned ventures, and perpetuated inefficient family control. Failure to develop the careful rationalization and cooperation of modern American management may only indicate a greater nearness to the days of agrarian-mercantile attitudes. The number of cases that have been accumulated in published research on Latin American business is too small to carry quantitative weight. The argument for cultural differentiation has to rest on accumulated observation and historical judgment as to norms. The scholars who have been most deeply immersed in these materials, would, I believe, be in substantial agreement that the examples cited illustrate widely shared traits of Latin culture, and I think that in a similar stage of industrialism these were not normal traits of United States culture.

In speculating upon the effect of these cultural differentials on economic growth, it is soon apparent that the impact varies with the type of activity, the size of business units, and the level of economic development. Evon Z. Vogt writes: "The widest proposition that I think can be defended with our present evidence is that the importance of value orientation in shaping the direction of change is proportional to the amount of economic and technological control a society has achieved."[26]

The highest level of such control is presumably found in United States big business run by professional management. Looking at this sector of the economy Paul F. Lazarsfeld notes that culture strongly influences the selection of matters for executive decision. He sees three factors influencing such personal decisions: "informal groups, the relation of statuses, and visibility."[27] As advanced management becomes ever more politically

[26] Evon Z. Vogt, "On the Concepts of Structure and Process in Cultural Anthropology," *American Anthropologist*, LXII (Feb. 1960), p. 266.
[27] Paul Lazarsfeld, "Reflections on Business," *American Journal of Sociology*, LXV (July 1959), p. 17.

and socially oriented and less concerned with technological problems the question arises according to Professor Lazarsfeld "whether sociological concepts like social visibility may not one day themselves become determinants of managerial activities."[28]

Obviously historians do not now have to confront these problems, but such thinking emphasizes the probability that the cultural characteristics favorable to growth at one level may differ significantly from those favorable at even a slightly higher level of complexity in business and social organization.

In Puerto Rico, for example, the traditional Spanish type of culture did not appear to impede the building of strong importing houses, moderate-sized sugar centrals, and successful small embroidery, ready-made clothing and furniture factories. Of these last three, only hand embroidery was sold on the mainland. Viewing the island market as a limited one that had to be divided among competitors, even sugar having a quota after 1934, entrepreneurs seldom took the risk of trying to expand.[29] Thus a small and fairly static business community could cultivate personal relations, eschew group activity and look for prestige outside the business world without running counter to the economic situation.

With the stimulation of manufacturing by the insular government from 1945 on, selling more products outside the Puerto Rican market became a possibility, and at the same time new technology and new marketing methods menaced the stability of the old internal arrangements. It was at this point that the lack of cooperative or group orientation began to appear as a hindrance to growth. Many sugar centrals had become uneconomically small, yet in spite of wide recognition of this fact there were no mergers as distinct from outright sales, of these family-owned mills.[30] Even more striking was the last ditch stand of small food wholesalers against the supermarkets and bigger distributors with better mainland connections. In Ponce in 1955, for example, there were 20 small wholesalers where two or three

[28] *Ibid.*, p. 19.
[29] Cochran, *Puerto Rican Businessman*, p. 162.
[30] This statement refers only to the period to 1956.

should have handled the business. But these entrepreneurs would not reconcile themselves to giving up their proprietorships by merging their interests with those of other families.

Granted that Puerto Rico was to become a mature industrial area these delays to the logical course of economic development illustrate not only the poor adjustment of Latin type individualism to the cooperative demands of mass production and distribution, but also the hindrances that a strong family system can impose on changes in the ownership of enterprise.

The dominant role of communication in economic development has been well recognized. Much of the writing of Harold A. Innis dealt with this theme. Arthur H. Cole makes changes in communication the basis for his stages of entrepreneurship.[31] Recently Richard L. Meier has said that change in the magnitude of economic factors, or growth, depends on "the flow of information and changes in the stage of informedness."[32] These, in turn, are closely related to other cultural characteristics. If people are industrially oriented they will absorb more and more technological learning, and progress accordingly, whereas if there is a lack of interest in such knowledge that rate of transfer may be too slow to affect economic change. Professor Gillin points out that in contrast to the normal pattern in the United States, Latin Americans have not been particularly receptive to ideas regarding technology.[33]

As has been emphasized, their attitudes regarding delegation of authority, free discussion in committees, and objective experi-

[31] Arthur H. Cole, "An Approach to the Study of Entrepreneurship: A Tribute to Edwin F. Gay," *The Journal of Economic History*, V, *Supplement* (1946), pp. 10 ff.

[32] Social Science Research Council, *Items*, XIV, 2 (June 1960), p. 16.

[33] John Gillin, "Ethos Components in Modern Latin American Culture," *American Anthropologist*, LVII (1955), 498. The reception pattern in the United States applies only to the more industrialized areas. For example, Texans of the land, cattle, and oil period, or roughly up to 1941, showed very little interest in general technical knowledge. Bankers did not try to learn about industrial risks, and Chambers of Commerce advised industrialists coming to Texas to bring their managers with them. See: Thomas C. Cochran, *The American Business System* (Cambridge: Harvard University Press, 1957; New York: Harper Torchbook edition, 1962), pp. 172 ff.

mentation with change also run counter to modern United States managerial concepts. Among seventy entrepreneurs in Puerto Rico only those who had prolonged schooling in the United States seemed able to make full transition to the attitudes current in advanced management.[34] Some of the northern-educated Puerto Ricans made only part of the transition. They talked the language of United States consultants but still reacted emotionally in the traditional patterns. Sometimes they displayed the fashionable United States type of personality at the office and the traditional Spanish type at home.

In Mexico "delegation may involve fundamental personality changes if it is to be effective."[35] Of the group of executives interviewed by Professor Fayerweather only two, "both of them young men who had rather exceptional educational experience, including extended stays in the United States, spoke intelligently about changes in their own attitudes. The rest were essentially lacking in what I shall call a learning attitude."[36] He calls the partial transition described above as "the formal behavior level of learning" as distinct from "alterations in basic attitudes."[37]

There are, of course, a number of elements not directly connected with particular types of personality that also affect the rate of transfer of information and attitudes. Three such factors are: the size of firms; the stage of technology; and the type of products available.

While the small entrepreneur has to be personally motivated to learn, the large firm can appoint a specialist to study new information. In 1950, for example, small businessmen in Puerto Rico had a tremendous amount of useful literature beamed at them by government and private agencies, but they paid little attention to it, taking their ideas from conversations with equally poorly informed fellow businessmen or necessarily biased traveling salesmen.[38] As might be expected, the lack of cooperative

[34] Cochran, *Puerto Rican Businessman*, pp. 143-44.
[35] Fayerweather, *Executive Overseas*, p. 20.
[36] *Ibid.*, p. 116.
[37] *Ibid.*, p. 119.
[38] Small businessmen in the United States are also hard to reach with new information, the difference is one of degree.

tendencies in Puerto Rican culture kept trade associations weak and their contributions to technical information slight. On the other hand, relatively big business firms kept in touch with the latest developments in the United States through frequent visits by both specialists and chief executives. In the big company studied in Argentina thirty-four trips by a wide range of executives were made to the United States during the single year 1958.

As a country reaches higher levels of technology with an almost inevitable increase in the size of firms the intake of outside information becomes greater, but its content is more complicated and more difficult to translate into practice. This proposition becomes obvious when comparing widely separated periods of industrial development. At an early period in industrialism the most advanced machines were not complex. In 1811 Francis Cabot Lowell surreptitiously observed English and Scotch power looms, and with the help of a good mechanic constructed satisfactory copies in the United States. In the 1930's college-educated Italian engineers in the large plant in Argentina were unable efficiently to produce sealed compressors for refrigeration even though they had United States blueprints to work from.

The transfer of knowledge regarding managerial practice appears, in part, to obey this same rule of increasing flow and increasing difficulty. In the 1830's ideas of efficient bank management could be acquired by talking to cashiers in London or other large banking centers. By the 1950's the largest Puerto Rican bank found it worthwhile to pay a firm of consultants from Chicago a very large fee for redesigning its system of management.

The acquisition of good working habits or "industrial discipline" in the lower ranks has been speeded by products that create new wants or goals. The Latin countries discussed here, and a large part of the world area classed as underdeveloped, lie in the tropical or subtropical zones. Warm climate and long growing seasons reduce the need among the working class for costly housing and special preparation for winter. Habits of accumulation appear to be less developed; leisure may seem preferable to the discipline of steady employment. In the twentieth century, however, new forms of consumer durables at prices that workers can meet if given long-term instalment credit, have changed tropical attitudes. Everywhere radios, televisions, refrigerators, washing machines, motor scooters, and automobiles have had great mass appeal. Like the Calvinistic force of doing God's work, desire for these objects converts idlers in the sun into machine tenders and office workers. The goals of the culture having been partially reshaped from preference for leisure to preference for consumer durables, the effect becomes cumulative.[39] Employees become more reliable and real wages rise; this, in turn, provides for larger consumption and makes the durables into more universal and mandatory marks of social prestige.[40] During the politico-economic confusions of the Péron regime this process was going on in Argentina, and was obvious during the same period in Puerto Rico.

IV

This discussion must be as unsatisfying and inconclusive as the present state of the analysis of culture and personality or of theories in social psychology. The aim has been to indicate by argument and example that the cultural elements that have to be included in any comprehensive approach to either economic growth or economic history can be analyzed.

From the material discussed, the following propositions may be offered regarding differences important for economic growth between United States and Latin American culture and personality. Comparatively the Latin American complex: 1) sacrifices rigorous economically directed effort, or profit maximization, to

[39] These durables have also altered culture in the developed temperate areas in ways that cannot be discussed here.

[40] Since history presents cases of partial and gradual although increasingly successful industrial development, I cannot altogether agree with W. W. Rostow's description of a take-off stage, or with Yusif A. Sayigh's observation that for sustained development an underdeveloped society must accept "the total challenge with its inevitable logic." W. W. Rostow, *The Stages of Economic Growth* (Cambridge: Cambridge University Press, 1960); Yusif A. Sayigh, "Innovating Enterprise and Development," Mimeo. for Center for International Affairs, Harvard University, December 7, 1959), p. 3.

family interests; 2) places social and personal emotional interests ahead of business obligations; 3) impedes mergers and other changes in ownership desirable for higher levels of technological efficiency and better adjustment to markets; 4) fosters nepotism to a degree harmful to continuously able top-management; 5) hinders the building up of a supply of competent and cooperative middle managers; 6) makes managers and workers less amenable to constructive criticism; 7) creates barriers of disinterest in the flow of technological communication; and 8) lessens the urge for expansion and risk-taking. These Latin qualities are not necessarily detriments to the good life, perhaps just the opposite, but they are hindrances to material progress under the Anglo-American concepts of a market-oriented capitalist economy.

As one inadequately versed in current economic and psychological hypotheses it would be presumptuous for me to say just how these elements should be utilized by theorists. Certain limitations, at least, seem apparent to the outsider. In spite of the work of Professor McClelland and others, measurement of these cultural differentials still seems rather remote. Yet, as qualities or tendencies they appear reliably identifiable. At present they suggest that the anticipated responses on which North Americans base economic or political activities may not be the same in Latin American or other countries. As against our inevitable desire to apply universal historical analogies and formulate general economic laws, to behave as though roles were played everywhere as in the United States, cultural differentials are warnings that each area will make its own amendments.

Lastly, the growing recognition of the inescapable importance of these basic cultural considerations may be ushering in a new period of the generalist in contrast to more than a generation of increased specialization. If so, the economic historian can hope that his methods of descriptive integration and tentative generalization may regain the prestige they enjoyed in the social science of the late nineteenth and early twentieth centuries. He may still lack answers or often fail to hit on the right question, but he has to work with all the variables and the result of their interaction as historical record.

VII: A Model for
Cultural Factors*

The need to work with all the variables does not preclude either economists or historians from developing explanatory models. The problem is to find those that will explain long-run norms of social behavior, and why they change. Many social science models for change are either conceived so broadly, as for example: "Change occurs when socially relevant new habits are acquired via a learning process," as to be blunt tools for analysis, or in order to provide detail introduce too many variables. Thus, in spite of the wide-recognition of the importance of social and cultural factors among both economists and historians, I know of no one who has successfully devised a comprehensive model.

I

A way out of this dilemma is to narrow the scope of the problem by focusing on a particular type of change where historical analogy can be of use. One such solution is to concentrate on how major variables affect the making of economic decisions. If every such decision was made by a computer into which social and economic factors were fed, or by different individuals each differently conditioned and differently placed in the social struc-

* Reprinted with permission from *Behavioral Science*.

ture, it would be useless to focus on the characteristics of the decision-maker. But fortunately this is not the case. In a given situation, decisions are normally made in sequence by the same man, who is not a random selection from the human species, but is, rather, a representative of a limited group in his culture. Thus the non-economic social factors come in a definable set of influences operating on the business decision-maker or entrepreneur.

As aggregates, entrepreneurs in a given type of activity represent certain ascertainable levels of education, social status, and types of cultural conditioning that produce a roughly definable modal personality. In making their decisions they play social roles anticipated by their associates and other groups in the culture. Therefore, in the modal entrepreneur, and in general the modes seem broad, there is a channel through which diverse and, in themselves, intangible social forces translate their effects into economic action; a point where social factors can be observed and estimated for relative intensities.

To begin with, executives' inner characters are largely conditioned by the type of child-rearing and schooling common to the culture. They receive the traditional admonitions, absorb the family attitudes of their class, learn the ideologies and conceptual schemes of the society. Latin American child-rearing, for example, even in the most advanced countries, tends to produce quite different characters from that of the United States.[1] Similarly, as seen in Chapter I, American child-rearing and schooling before about 1920 produced differently conditioned individuals than did that of the 1920's and 1930's.[2] As explained in Chapter I, it seems reasonable to suppose that after about 1920 a generation of entrepreneurs were being trained with fewer fixed values, less secure principles, greater tendencies to be influenced by those around them: in a word, to be good organization men.

Whether this shift has been advantageous to the business community or not, it is probably too early to say, but it has fitted in

[1] David Landy, *Tropical Childhood* (Chapel Hill: University of North Carolina Press, 1959) , pp. 238 ff.
[2] See footnote references in Chapter I.

with the needs of large scale mass-production for a cooperative team-like type of entrepreneurship. One that is in quite striking contrast to the individual-and-family-centrism of less industrially advanced areas.

Returning to our model of the entrepreneurial situation, the business executive, therefore, plays a social role partly shaped by the modal type of personality that comes from the social conditioning of his generation. While unusual characters will always depart from the norms, in general, invention, and innovation will tend to be along lines congenial to the entrepreneur's type of conditioning. Anthropologists interested in change support this premise by saying that new items in the culture must be not only physically but also psychologically available. Subjective constructions of the items must be made and these will depend on the value orientations of the culture.[3] The rate of change will be a function of the rate of subjective construction. Thus entrepreneurs in one culture will conceptualize and use a new item, and in another culture where the item is equally available they may remain indifferent to its existence.

Because entrepreneurial roles are defined by the ideas of those important to the success of the actor, in many new pursuits such as manufacturing in an underdeveloped country, the defining groups, those whom the entrepreneur seeks to satisfy, are often not connected with the industrial operation, per se. A role is established, therefore, that is not necessarily instrumental to the task involved. There is also much operational trial and error. An Argentine manufacturer of the 1920's, for example, wished primarily to become an important family, business and civic leader —achievements not necessarily functional to his role as an entrepreneur. In operating a pioneer big business he had no guide as to how he should divide his time between production, finance, sales and government contacts. He could only learn by experience how little working capital and what amount of time obligations would be safe. But in well established corporations such

[3] Evon Z. Vogt, "On the Concepts of Structure and Process in Cultural Anthropology," *American Anthropologist*, LXII (1960), p. 255. As used in this book, the term entrepreneur is synonymous with executive and implies no special propensity for innovation.

as the railroads discussed in Chapter VIII, defining groups such as the senior officers or the board have well-formed expectations and the entrepreneurial role will be closely defined.

It is obvious that the primarily cultural factors operating on the personality of the entrepreneur and the defining of his role by those involved, must accommodate to some degree to the necessities of the operations to be carried out. But the accommodation does not have to be an efficient one. For example, in West Texas in 1950 industrial risks in new lines such as furniture and other home fittings were relatively safe and offered high rates of return, but the banker role, as defined by both fellow officers and directors, was to loan only on cattle or land, and consequently the latter role was not efficiently adjusted to the actual needs or opportunities of the situation.[4]

This relatively simple framework of an entrepreneurial role defined by the personality of the actor, the expectations of groups with power to sanction deviations from expected behavior, and the operational needs of the function to be performed, subsumes all the social or cultural factors. But, obviously, when so much is fitted into so little, each category must, and does cover many complications.[5]

For example, observation of cultures making the change from agricultural trading communities to industrial states shows that family obligations are one of the chief dysfunctional elements. But the force of a feeling of obligation in the entrepreneur to the members of an extended family is hard to measure. It is easy enough to say that professional middle management will only arise as this obligation grows weaker, but where are the critical points? How dysfunctional must this hold-over from the static agrarian family become, before a major alteration will occur in the entrepreneurial role?

It is because such questions, involving a variety of uncontrollable variables, cannot be directly answered by purely theo-

[4] Thomas C. Cochran, *The American Business System* (Cambridge: Harvard University Press, 1957; Harper Torchbook edition, 1962), pp. 173-174.
[5] See Leland H. Jenks, "The Role Structure of Entrepreneurial Personality," *Change and the Entrepreneur* (Cambridge: Harvard University Press, 1949), pp. 108-152.

retical analysis that history becomes useful. The only plausible answers that can be offered have to be in terms of analogies taken from various historic situations. Once factors are defined, as in the entrepreneurial role model, it is possible to collect tolerably comparable data for such situations. Whether the facts are collected by economists or historians, whether the time span is two months or twenty years, it is still an historical type of data; it is the record of what appears to have happened in a real situation where the variable could not be controlled to fit a research design. Thus John Fayerweather's *The Executive Overseas,* a study based chiefly on intimate observation of a small number of executives in Mexico over a four-month period, is a history, even though the time-span is short and the data is unconventional.[6]

It is easier to demonstrate the dynamics of the entrepreneurial model by selecting instances from abroad where the pressures of advanced American technology have rapidly penetrated traditional agricultural cultures, but I believe there will be more novelty in selecting some examples of entrepreneurial interaction with change from American history. In the last 150 years businessmen have participated in three changes that cannot be neglected in any account of how we arrived at where we are: first, the rapid adoption of industrial machinery in the first half of the nineteenth century; second, the rise of professional management in the large corporation, starting in the second half of the century; and third, the rationalization of mass production techniques in the twentieth century. In each of these major changes the social factors in American culture operating through the entrepreneur appear to be well marked.

II

In turning to the first type of change, it is striking that the usual problem of the present day growth theorist is to account for overly slow industrial expansion either in some less advanced

[6] Syracuse: Syracuse University Press, 1959.

area or in the present United States, whereas in studying early nineteenth-century America the problem is to account for unusually rapid industrialization with novel characteristics. A major question is why did American executives adopt machinery more rapidly than their counterparts in Western Europe? And the most convincing economic answer is because of a shortage of labor. H. J. Habakkuk recently made an extensive analysis of this problem of labor shortage in relation to early American manufacturing methods, and came to the general conclusion that the development of the latter can be deduced from purely economic circumstances.[7] In his arguments he sees certain entrepreneurial characteristics as products of the American economic environment. This involves a chicken-egg problem, and my position is that if a modal personality trait exists at a given time it is more realistic to treat it as a cultural factor, regardless of what may have accounted for this trait historically.

While not contradicting any of Professor Habakkuk's economic reasoning, the position taken by John E. Sawyer, in an article in 1954, that factors of culture and social structure were extremely important in early American manufacturing seems to offer a more useful explanation, one applicable beyond manufacturing to other fields of entrepreneurial activity.

Using the work of both these scholars let us see how their conclusions fit our model of entrepreneurial role. The American situation emphasized certain operational needs. Since labor was scarce and valuable there was a greater inducement to plan for its efficient use. This in turn led to greater consciousness of costs and alertness to opportunities for substituting machinery, in other words, to rapid subjective construction of such new items. Habakkuk finds a contrast to England in these respects, and the contrast with Latin America or a nation like Greece would be even more striking.

But American entrepreneurial behavior also depended on different attitudes in the defining groups such as employees, fellow managers, customers and bankers. Innovations within what an-

_____

[7] *American and British Technology* (New York: Cambridge University Press, 1952), pp. 126 ff.

thropologists have called the "limits of sameness" met relatively little resistance. That is, if the innovation promised the same general type of product at less cost it was likely to be considered rationally, on economic grounds rather than resisted by either proprietors or labor from disinclination toward change. These matters, of course, are relative. W. P. Strassmann has emphasized early American resistance to risking additional capital. One can only say that, comparatively, Habakkuk finds British investors still more cautious, and in the nations destined to remain underdeveloped, the resistance was great enough to check almost all large scale industrial investment.

American customers placed little value on fine craftsmanship—for that they would buy imports. In domestic goods they sought cheapness and utility. There was also a noticeable feeling that expenditure to produce exceptionally long life or permanence in an article was a waste. The migratory American purchaser would often sell his equipment before a subsequent move to another locality, or replace it by something better.

As far as the general public was concerned the businessman was playing to an appreciative audience. Trade or manufacturing, even on a small scale, carried no social stigma. Financial success could immediately raise the businessman to the top level of most American society. This pull of unrestricted opportunity was absent in the more rigid societies which characterized the rest of the civilized world.

These attitudes on the part of defining groups were necessarily reflected in the personality of the entrepreneur. Thus the entrepreneurs of New England and the Middle States in the first half of the nineteenth century seem to have shared a feeling that work was a duty, and that a calling should be carefully selected and vigorously pursued. Child-rearing and education both placed emphasis on the busy, productive individual. An optimism about getting ahead was emphasized in the school texts, and presumably in family conversation.[8]

[8] See Richard de Charms and Gerald H. Moeller, "Values Expressed in American Childrens Readers, 1800-1950," *Journal of Abnormal and Social Psychology*, 64 (1962), pp. 136-142.

Inadequate though it was, elementary education was relatively widespread and more business oriented in New England and the Middle States than elsewhere in the world. Governor DeWitt Clinton of New York illustrated a common cultural attitude when he said in 1826: "The first duty of government, and the surest evidence of good government, is the encouragement of education."[9] Of entrepreneurs born between 1790 and 1819 who came to be listed in the *Dictionary of American Biography*, C. Wright Mills found a total of 55 per cent with high school education or more, and only 23 per cent with only apprenticeship or a negligible formal education.[10] Of manufacturing entrepreneurs between 1789 and 1865, whose education is recorded in company histories, Thomas B. Brewer also found 55 per cent with high school or college education and only 7 per cent with no formal education.[11]

There are many characteristics of both the personality of executives and the attitudes or expectations of defining groups that appear to be associated with the highly migratory character of American population. Unfortunately there are few reliable statistics back of 1850, but the case studies that exist suggest that the average American moved several times during his life, and that businessmen were probably more geographically mobile than the average. The elements associated with migration that would increase the efficiency of an entrepreneurial role were: emphasis on self-help as against aid from family status; willingness to cooperate with relative strangers, or impersonality; tolerance of, and adjustment to, strange conditions; and the almost inevitable tendency to innovate in making such adjustments.[12] Recent studies have underlined the importance of even

[9] Quoted in Elwood P. Cubberley, *Public Education in the United States* (Boston: Houghton Mifflin, 1919), p. 112.

[10] C. Wright Mills, "The American Business Elite: A Collective Portrait, "*The Journal of Economic History*, V, Supplement (1945).

[11] Thomas B. Brewer, "The Formative Period of 140 Manufacturing Companies, 1789-1929," (Microfilm Thesis, University of Pennsylvania, 1962), p. 49.

[12] See Everett S. Lee, "The Turner Thesis Reexamined," *American Quarterly*, XIII (Spring, 1961), pp. 77-83.

moderate changes in environment in stimulating new ideas and practices.[13]

One recognizes the above list as containing the elements that scholars have associated with successful industrialization. Cooperation and impersonality have been rated as specially important factors.[14] In the 1830's de Toqueville was impressed with American cooperativeness. In contrast to other cultures where pride in family companies has led to failure to meet changing market situations rationally, early American executives engineered mergers, formed associations to control prices and production, and in general demonstrated a rational ability to put profits ahead of personal rivalries or animosities.[15] Impersonality, keeping friendships apart from business dealings, has led Americans to expect market considerations to govern patronage. There have been, of course, exceptions to this, but in general suppliers are changed for business reasons with a readiness not present in more traditional societies.[16]

From the early nineteenth century on American managers showed what Albert O. Hirschman has called the " 'growth perspective,' which comprises not only the desire for economic growth but also the perception of the essential nature of the road leading toward it."[17] On the basis of the rapid and creative subjective construction induced by American conditioning, whatever its original causes, the role of the entrepreneur becomes a major differentiating element in social and economic change. In spite of a level of technological knowledge below that of England, even in 1850, the American entrepreneur introduced a more highly mechanized industrialism and set in motion an upward spiral of labor-saving devices which continued to operate.[18]

[13] H. G. Barnett, *Innovation: The Basis of Cultural Change* (New York; McGraw Hill, 1953) , pp. 87, 88, 93.

[14] Albert O. Hirschman, *The Strategy of Economic Development* (New Haven: Yale University Press, 1958), p. 17.

[15] See Thomas C. Cochran, *The Puerto Rican Businessman* (Philadelphia: University of Pennsylvania Press, 1959) , pp. 91, 96.

[16] John E. Sawyer, "The Social Basis of the American System of Manufacturing," *The Journal of Economic History*, XIV, (1954), pp. 365-366.

[17] Hirschman, *Strategy*, p. 10.

[18] Sawyer, "American System," pp. 365-366.

III

The second type of entrepreneurially guided change, the replacing of the owner entrepreneur by the professional executive as the chief managerial type, has probably been the most important development in American business, and surely one of the major changes in American culture. The need for re-adapting the attitudes of certain defining groups, chiefly officers and directors, and altering the role of the chief entrepreneurs to meet the demands and opportunities of the large, widely-owned, corporation inevitably brought about fundamental change. Whereas in our first example changes in operations appear to have been accelerated by the peculiar conditioning of American entrepreneurs, in this second example a change in the methods of business operation gradually alters the role and the personality of the entrepreneur. It should be emphasized, however, that these American entrepreneurs were peculiarly susceptible to role changes in the directions needed for the functioning of the large corporation.

Between 1850 and 1890, most of the new obligations and opportunities associated with administering other people's money were worked out in the large railroads.[19] In the 1850's, officers and directors saw nothing amiss in being on both sides of a bargain, of selling supplies to the railroad, buying land from the road for resale at a profit, or of owning facilities such as bridges or stockyards that the road had to rent. Some of these arrangements had arisen because the early railroads were chronically short of capital, and as conditions became easier after 1865 ethics grew stricter. In the best run companies, by the mid-1880's the executive role had been defined with a strictness that has not greatly altered since that time. In 1883 Charles E. Perkins, President of the Chicago Burlington and Quincy Railroad wrote to one of his top executives: "The smallest kind of an

[19] See Chapter V.

interest in a coal mine would be objectionable." Officers should
not "make money out of side shows.[20]

As important as the improvement in ethics, essential to the
continued attraction of capital, was the development of modern
systems of big business management. Advancement on the basis
of ability, security of tenure, delegation of authority, decen-
tralizations of operations, open but orderly channels of communication and managerial cooperation for company welfare may all
seem at first glance to be inevitable adjustments to the problem
of size. But anyone who has studied the functioning of large organizations in other cultures knows this is not so. Until very recent years the biggest electrica lmachinery manufacturing firm in
Latin America failed, in spite of the services of United States
management consultants, to develop these characteristics.[21] Delegation of authority, easy communication between levels of management, and cooperation among managers on the same level
have all been difficult to achieve in Latin America, and in most
other cultures. Even in England and Germany there is more
difficulty in these respects than in the United States.

The decisive difference appears to be that American business
leaders have been reared in the equalitarian atmosphere of an
out-going, pragmatic, democratic society. They have been taught
from childhood onwards that cooperation for mutual benefit is
good, and the type of individualism they develop does not stand
in the way of easy relations with their peers.

This latter point is of particular importance. As the result of
rather elaborate analyses of United States individualism in
comparison to that of Latin America some basically important
differences appear. Dr. Fayerweather calls Mexican executives
"individualistic" in personality and Americans "group-oriented."[22] To the former he attaches the characteristics of: distrust
in the relations of managers with their superiors; hostility in

[20] Thomas C. Cochran, *Railroad Leaders, 1845-1890,* (Cambridge: Harvard
University Press, 1953), pp. 117, 436.
[21] Thomas C. Cochran and Ruben E. Reina, *Entrepreneurship in Argentine Culture* (Philadelphia: University of Pennsylvania Press, 1962), pp. 184-
191, 222-225.
[22] Fayerweather, *Executive,* pp. 12-17, 194-195.

relations with their peers; and a sense of separation in their relations with subordinates. To the group-oriented personality he attributes confidence and fellow-feeling in relations with superiors and peers, and a sense of union with subordinates. Research at the University of Pennsylvania has indicated that so-called American individualism is a matter of standing up for one's rights in the group or against government or other external encroachment in contrast to the more subjective, inward-looking individualism of Latin Americans.[23]

As seen in the previous chapter, the Latin type of personality, shared to some degree by businessmen in most underdeveloped areas, has made it much more difficult to create efficient managerial structures for expanding business; or viewed another way, has tended to put a ceiling on corporate expansion at the level where one man or a small family group can give personal attention to the details of operation. In contrast to Latin distrust of fellow executives, the British missions sent between 1949 and 1952 to observe American manufacturing methods issued reports such as: "Among the executives we met, we encountered . . . a readiness to encourage and pass on knowledge to juniors."[24] The United States attitudes have accelerated change through expansion, mergers, diversification of products, and decentralization.[25]

IV

Economists tend to see the third major change, the rapid spread of advanced mass-production techniques, as a function of both the state of technology and the size of the American domestic market. Since, by 1900, the United States had more and wealthier customers than either England or Germany it

---

[23] See Cochran, *Puerto Rican Businessman,* pp. 122-125.
[24] Sawyer, "American System," p. 365.
[25] See Alfred D. Chandler, *Structure and Strategy* (Cambridge: Massachusetts Institute of Technology Press, 1962).

developed larger-scale processes and bigger companies. But social historians are impressed by additional factors.

To begin with, American culture as expressed in law and government demanded efforts to maintain the ideal of competition. The interpretation of restraint of trade by the courts, and by the anti-trust laws of states and nation, deprived medium sized businesses of the ability to protect their positions by legal agreements or cartels. This led to mergers into larger units which were judged legal as long as they did not try to, or threaten to, monopolize the trade. The bigger units resulting from this social pressure would perhaps have led, in any case, to a more intensive search for economies of scale than seems to have been pursued elsewhere. But in addition to these exogenous forces that altered the operational demands of the entrepreneurial role, the personality characteristics noted in early American manufacturers persisted. The English missions of the mid-twentieth century reported that productivity,

is part of the American way of life, an article of faith as much as a matter of economics . . . Americans believe it is their mission to lead the world in productive efficiency.

'Cost-consciousness' . . . does not simply mean cutting costs . . . It also means not missing opportunities.

American managements look continually towards the future. They base their decisions on an intelligent anticipation of trends rather than wait until the pressure of current events forces them to make the decisions."[26]

Henry Ford, generally credited with being the most dramatic adapter of new mass-production techniques in the twentieth century, shows interesting contrasts to the man who, more nearly than any other, was his counterpart in Argentina. Ford was chiefly interested in efficiency and machinery or, in anthropological language, oriented toward change in mechanical items. His subjective constructions were in terms of new machines and processes.[27] Although each of his major innovations, Model T,

[26] Sawyer, "American System," p. 365.
[27] Allan Nevins, Ford (New York: Charles Scribner's Sons, 1954), I, pp. 49 ff.

the power driven continuous assembly line, and the five-dollar minimum wage can readily be attributed to the ideas of subordinates, Ford saw his entrepreneurial role in terms of these achievements. On the other hand, Torcuato Di Tella, while introducing household electric refrigeration and other electrical machinery to Argentina, saw his role in much broader terms, and delegated most of the purely technological work to trusted subordinates. In other words, Ford represented the classic American drives for mechanization and efficiency, Di Tella the Latin interests in the all-around social man who would be family leader, business leader, intellectual and patron of the arts. Both were extremely "driven" individuals but Ford had the singleness of purpose so usual to American entrepreneurial personality, Di Tella the more diffused ambitions of men of Latin and many other cultures.

V

So far, little has been said about elements in the social structure, as distinct from values, that may negate change. Most such elements are associated with rigidities. Their existence, however, is usually manifest in the conditioning of the modal entrepreneurial personality. An aristocratic social structure like nineteenth-century England, for example, made becoming an aristocrat a more attractive goal for the successful entrepreneur than continued expansion of his business. This structure tended to produce a cut-off point in expansion similar to that imposed by the limits of direct personal or family control.

Aside from caste or status lines, per se, some cultures are no doubt more static and ceremonial than others. While these conditions might be traced back to geographical and economic circumstances, at any specific time they are given parts of the situation. Fear of change by the power elite, for example, may be based on low energy and resources, but it comes to exist as a separate factor.

The general position taken here, as distinct from the specific applications of the role model, is well summed up in technical language by psychologists de Charms and Moeller. They say: "We propose that motivation, or cultural orientation be conceived as an intervening variable standing between antecedent environmental factors associated with economic and political changes and consequent behavior resulting in cultural changes such as technological growth. . . . Thus two cultures undergoing similar economic or political change may react quite differently due to intervening variables of values, child rearing practices, and motives."[28]

The role model offers ways of defining and organizing these "intervening variables." But, unfortunately, neither this nor other current systems can quantify the variables so that additions or subtractions can be made in the measurable terms of land, labor, capital or market price. One cannot speak of units or doses of personality or values. For problems of change over time where the variables are numerous and non-quantifiable there seems no substitute for historical analogy applied to carefully defined situations. Location of social variables in terms of more or less, or below or above some norm, or as correlates of other variables is frequently possible. These operations do not lead to equations but rather to propositions stating probable relationships. David McClelland's statement that limits are placed on motivation for achievement by "too large discrepancies between expectations and results," which "may develop an avoidance motive as far as achievement is concerned";[29] or Evon J. Vogt's proposition, stated in the preceding chapter, that "the importance of value orientation in shaping the direction of change is proportional to the amount of economic and technological control a society has achieved";[30] examples of useful, but non-quantifiable relationships. They are, however, of the same

[28] de Charms and Moeller, "Values," p. 142.

[29] David C. McClelland, John W. Atkinson, Russell A. Clark, Edgard L. Lowell, *The Achievement Motive* (New York: Appleton-Century-Crofts, 1953), p. 65.

[30] Evon Z. Vogt, "On the Concepts of Structure and Process in Cultural Anthropology," *American Anthropologist*, LXII (1960), p. 266.

degree of specificity as such economic maxims as "the larger the market the greater the division of labor."

Role theory allows for change by the deviant action of an individual, but the emphasis in this discussion has been on change as the interaction of modal types of personality with the culturally conditioned expectations of defining groups and the operational needs of situations. Exogenous changes in population, resources, technology, consumer demand or merely what Willard Hurst has called "cumulative institutional drift," all seem likely to impinge first on the role structure by creating new operational needs, but the entrepreneurial response to these needs may be a succesful innovation or dogged continuance of a dysfunctional way of doing things.[31] The response will depend on variables of personality and culture, which, as we have seen, are predictable with certain limits.

There is no theoretical reason why important innovation in role behavior could not arise from inner-conditioning independently of all immediate exogenous factors. But historical observation suggests that such instances are rare. It may be, for example, that the particular innovations credited to Ford would only have been prompted in the precise year by such a uniquely conditioned character, but over a twenty-year span the exact timing seems relatively unimportant. The given innovations or superior ones usually seem to be in process of introduction by several entrepreneurs. A general theory for relating economic and other social factors to change should deal with normal responses of functional groups to, at least, partially repetitive situations. From this standpoint a model of entrepreneurial role is a useful device.

[31] Willard Hurst, *Law and the Social Process* (Ann Arbor: University of Michigan Press, 1962), pp. 80-81.

VIII: The Social Role
of Railroad Leaders

Research in the business correspondence of the presidents of eight railroads between 1845 and 1890 was started in advance of the historian's use of role theory. The policy or attitude statements from some 10,000 of the 100,000 letters examined were not extracted to fit such hypotheses.[1] Instead, social role was adopted *post facto* as a theory that fit the collected evidence. In fact, had we never been supplied with the formal statements of role theory by Theodore M. Newcomb, Leland H. Jenks and others, some similar propositions might have emerged from efforts to give meaning to the data.[2]

The initial problem was the historical value of statements that might be deliberately misleading. The Chinese have a proverb to the effect that language is used to conceal intentions. Certainly no series of letters, whether from clergymen, politicians, or businessmen can be taken uniformly at face value. But how may statements be discounted or interpreted in such a way that one may draw some type of general meaning from them?

Usually the letters of one man are used in connection with the preparation of a biography of their author or the detailed analysis of a series of his actions. In either case cumulative

---

[1] Rosamond B. Cochran and I jointly did this research.

[2] See: Leland H. Jenks, "The Role Structure of Entrepreneurial Personality," in *Change and the Entrepreneur* (Cambridge: Harvard University Press, 1949), pp. 108-152; and Neal Gross, Ward S. Mason and Alexander W. McEadwin, *Explorations in Role Analysis* (New York: John Wiley, 1958).

knowledge of the writer's idiosyncrasies, continuing motivation, and, most of all, his actions themselves provide clues to acceptable interpretations. But when one reads the letters of a large group of men engaged over the course of many years in a common occupation, all of these conventional indicators are lacking. More specifically, what reliable information regarding entrepreneurial ideas may be gained from the letters of some sixty men having the same type of status.

The letters were not a truly representative sample. Railroads and officers were selected from each part of the country, but available correspondence files ultimately gave a disproportionate place to northern roads. Furthermore, the well-managed roads, untainted by scandal, seem to have been the ones most inclined to preserve their executive correspondence and to give scholars access to it. Consequently, the selection contains none of the letters of major roads controlled by notorious speculators. Aside from these two limitations, the 100,000-odd letters read have offered detailed and presumably representative information on general social and business attitudes as well as on railroad policy.

Returning to the problem of extracting reliable generalizations from the mass of evidence, it was obvious that knowledge of the inner character of each of sixty men would be too superficial to be reliable, and the analysis of the action involved in each instance would lead to a shelf of histories. We were forced, therefore, either to find some new technique of evaluation or else to admit that 100,000 personal letters were, taken by themselves, relatively useless as historical evidence.

In searching for defensible assumptions that would give order and meaning to statements of executives, it appeared that there were certain uniformities of idea and attitude that arose from the fact that the letters were all from men writing in their status as railroad executives. If these uniformities could be defined and hypotheses found that provided a general explanation for such regularities as the letters contained, the project would add somewhat to the small supply of tools for the interpretation of intellectual and social history.

I

The effort to define uniformities in attitude soon showed that such uniformities arose partly because certain business situations presented few alternatives. The fixed elements in the market for capital or product, the expressed aim of profit, the rigidities of bureaucratic structures, and a dozen other similar factors might leave only one or two possible answers to a problem. For example, no matter how much an aggressive professional manager might wish to expand his road during a depression, he had to face the fact that the hard-pressed capitalists would not invest at such a time.[3] Therefore, the record of decisions regarding "counter-cyclical" investment mirrors the limitation of alternatives more than the understanding of the entrepreneur.

But there were uniformities in attitude that had to be ascribed to other forces acting upon the executives. Some of these were obviously the uniform sanctions of the society, the adages, admonitions, social ceremonies, and traditional practices by which society seeks to protect itself from unpredictable behavior. Such pressures for conformity generally shaped the business decisions. Consequently, in situations affected by strong sanctions, such as the expectation that executives should strive to make profits for their company, we should expect a high degree of uniformity of opinion. Executives, moreover, generally knew the preconceived ideas of people important to them in a business way and consciously or unconsciously strove to live up to such expectations.

With the discovery of role theory it was soon clear that the characteristics of the railroad data added-up to a well-defined social role. Success in the status of top-executive in a large corporate hierarchy depended directly upon the approval of certain other people. And these defining groups were easily located. The evidence showed that the opinions of fellow top executives, of the members of the board of directors, and particularly of the principal general entrepreneurs on the board,

---

[3] A "professional" manager is one with no large investments in the securities of the road.

were the ones that most strongly influenced the executive role.[4] In so far as the management interest might occasionally conflict with the investment interest this was not a completely homogeneous group. But differences in attitude were infrequent. Usually all saw the executive role in much the same terms, because managers recognized that the general entrepreneurs, the men with access to capital, were the ones who controlled railroad careers and who could grant the favors that brought wealth and prestige. And among these men themselves the opinions of their peers counted for more than those of anyone else.

Therefore, no matter whom a railroad executive addressed in business correspondence, whether politician, clergyman, or shipper, he tended to write in terms acceptable to his company group. Aside from internal evidence of this characteristic in the letters themselves, it should follow from the fact that once a letter left the office there was no foreseeing its ultimate use. It might be quoted in committee hearings, or newspapers, or referred back to influential directors. This could be summed up by saying that at this time the directors of a company still directed, and that even presidents wrote business letters acceptable to their bosses. From this it also follows that the statements of employees of big business companies, at any executive level, should illustrate particularly well the characteristics of a common social role.

The pervasive bias in group expression suggested by the concept of social role colored but did not altogether inhibit the expression of individual feelings. A religious humanitarian, for example, might urge better treatment of the working man, and raise money for railroad Y.M.C.A.'s, but he would try to explain his actions in ways not contradictory to the prevailing business philosophy. Such deviation suggests, but does not confirm, a range of acceptable attitudes in that part of the social role.

Another type of individual expression occurs in areas where the social role is undefined. Railroad presidents were not expected

[4] By general entrepreneur we mean a man who exercised an important influence in many companies by virtue of his command of capital, and who ordinarily held no office beyond that of director, or chairman of the board.

to have any set group attitudes toward subjects such as slavery in the territories, or closer ties with Canada. A man could be for or against either one without seriously violating any of the general sanctions as to what was proper. In such areas of expression, therefore, it seems reasonable to suppose that the writer expressed his own ideas, save as a pro-slavery president might avoid the subject altogether in writing to an anti-slavery chairman.

At the opposite pole from purely individual opinions are statements of company policy. Here the executive speaks his own mind only to the degree that were he utterly opposed to company policy he would presumably have to resign. Such policy statements, being the result of group deliberation, should reflect the social role quite accurately and directly. But the hypotheses of social roles and sanctions give a strong basis for supposing that if any one railroad entrepreneur reacted to a situation in a certain way others with similar conditioning and knowledge should react similarly. Or to state the converse, the odds should be against any particular type of statement in a common situation being peculiar to the individual.

It is not essential that society be seen this way in order to accept the tentative conclusion drawn from the letters. Social role has been used because it offers a defined and consistent, rather than a vague explanation for common attitudes that have been previously accounted for in other terms. The concept seems particularly applicable to the corporation with its well-defined controlling groups. The generalizations set forth here are not, therefore, observations about nineteenth-century businessmen as a whole, but only about the ideas and attitudes of executives in large corporations. Role, for example, explains some of the "why" of behavior directed toward the conservation of capital by non-capitalists, some of the psychological rigidity associated with bureaucratic structures, some of the calculated, impersonal conduct of managers, and some of the drive for company expansion. Ideally, the recognition of a well-defined role should allow fairly accurate forecasting of executive conduct.

II

Re-examination of the evidence for role analysis brought out a number of major characteristics; as might be expected, there were relatively few differences in opinion in the letters on matters of routine business, on subjects, that is, where the role had been well defined.[5] A pervasive element in the role was respect for superiors, or, in the case of the top-most financiers, their regard for the opinion of their peers. Such sensitivity to the prerogatives of place and seniority is probably a necessity of hierarchical structures.

The executive's associates, his major defining group, expected him to be well informed and logical. No artistic temperament or what John Murray Forbes referred to as a "queer, vague vein about the blood" was wanted in these men of topmost business responsibility. There was a premium on exact, terse expression. In a period given to fanciful and ornate writing, the lean and pointed phraseology of these business letters is striking. Compare, for example, James F. Joy's "These are times when bold action is the only safe action and in this daring action the Southern Company have shown themselves wise,"[6] with this roughly contemporaneous observation by the famous clergyman and writer William Ellery Channing: "These are periods when the principles of experience need to be modified, when hope and trust and instinct claim a share with prudence in the guidance of affairs, when, in truth to dare is the highest wisdom."[7] Although about 40 per cent of the railroad leaders had attended college, and most of them came from prosperous families of the areas in which learning was most highly regarded, they permitted

[5] The homogeneity in social and geographical origins of the officer-director groups probably added to the role's clear and uniform features. The process of defining a role might be a more difficult one with, let us say, politicians, where the social background of the men and the reference and defining groups would be broader and less homogeneous.

[6] James F. Joy to Erastus Corning, January 21, 1851 (Erastus Corning Collection, Albany Institute of History and Art).

[7] William E. Channing, "The Union," *The Works of William E. Channing* (Boston: American Unitarian Association, 1892), p. 641.

themselves few digressions from the business at hand. They either could not, or did not seek to embellish their prose with allusions to literature, art, or scholarly knowledge.

Since the representatives of large investing interests were the most important individuals in defining the role, it is not surprising that "the company" was identified with the major stockholders rather than with the employees, and that company welfare was measured in earnings. It also follows logically, as well as from the evidence, that strict care of property rights and respect for wealth, were essential elements in the role.

The good business executive was the man who kept his personal sentiments and emotions out of his work—the man who decided all questions on the basis of how they would affect the long-run welfare and stability of the company. "Your first duty and mine also," wrote President Watrous of the New York, New Haven and Hartford "is to the property with which we are respectively connected and we have no duty or right, even, to sacrifice that for anything or anybody."[8] Fairly wide latitude was permitted in the selection of ways of performing one's duty to the company, provided the practices were not of a type disapproved by the eastern financial interests, and the chances of legal penalties were not too great.

Since the railroad was under social and political pressure from its earliest days, ideas soon developed on how managers should conduct external relations. Believing that the public lacked understanding of railroad problems, in doubtful cases executives and directors favored secrecy. They also believed that nothing would be gained by granting public favors at the expense of revenue. Requests for aid from schools, churches and similar institutions were to be judged strictly in terms of their direct effect on the welfare of the company. "Our mission," explained John W. Brooks of the Burlington and Missouri River, Nebraska, "is not that of aiding institutions of learning or religion because they commend themselves to our personal judgment. . . .

[8] G. D. Watrous to J. H. Wilson, November 29, 1882 (Archives of New York, New Haven, and Hartford Railroad, New Haven, Connecticut).

We can properly help . . . when it is clearly for the advantage of our stockholders to do so."[9]

Managers were expected to be particularly wary in dealing with politicians. There was no uniform role prescription for the proper relations of business and government, but the firmly held premise that what business did was economic and developed the country while government action was usually negative and parasitical, gave businessmen the feeling of having virtue on their side. As Leland H. Jenks has put it, the railroad leader "considered himself an agent of civilization, an embodiment of collective enterprise."[10] There were many instances in which the influencing of political action by the railroad management or the disregard of laws pending their testing by the courts were regarded as the proper and moral course. For example, Forbes took a tolerant view of Oakes Ames' bribery of Congressmen in the Credit Mobilier scandal: "The Road was better built—quicker—and did work better than such a plan promised or would have been accomplished under any but so strong and energetic a head as Ames." Forbes added, "I have always tried to avert blame from him for the mistakes he made."[11] In this, as in similar cases, good material ends appeared to justify the questionable means.

The aspects of the role discussed so far involved neither important conflicts nor changes over the period, they were aspects that the executive accepted as a matter of course, as part of the way people should normally think and act in American society. But there was no conventional answer to the problem of how certain personal interests of the executive affected his devotion to the financial welfare of the company. In the early years the conception of the role favored a wide latitude on the part of both executives and directors to engage in private ventures connected with constructing the road, or selling it land, materials,

[9] J. W. Brooks to G. Harris, March 9, 1871 (Archives of the Chicago, Burlington and Quincy Railroad, Newberry Library, Chicago, Illinois).
[10] "Railroads as an Economic Force," *The Journal of Economic History*, IV, May 1944, p. 10.
[11] J. M. Forbes to J. B. Sanborn, June 10, 1878 (Archives of Chicago, Burlington & Quincy Railroad, Newberry Library, Chicago, Illinois).

and equipment. This leeway was perhaps a carry-over from an age of small-owner-managed enterprises and a reflection of the direct participation of the general entrepreneurs in such "sidelines." But as time went on and the leading directors became less active in the affairs of the road, the conflict of many of these managerial ventures with the best interests of the railroad company became more apparent to them, and such activity was condemned. By 1885, for example, Charles E. Perkins, President of the Burlington, wrote a fellow executive that "The smallest kind of interest in a coal mine would be objectionable."[12]

III

Some of the limits of role definition may be illustrated by taking a case where the individual's own desires ran contrary to the executive role. The control of wages by the law of supply and demand, a generally held business concept, was a positively sanctioned attitude of the role. Robert Harris, while president of C.B. and Q., personally questioned the wisdom of the rigorous application of this idea. At the time of the railroad strikes of 1877 he wrote Director Forbes: "Perhaps we may be able to devise a plan for increasing the pay of employees contingent upon net earnings. . . ."[13] And a week later he wrote his fellow executive, Perkins, "I do not think the Company should confine its observations to the single point—what is the least price at which labor can be had?"[14] But he sought to reconcile his unconventional attitude with the regard for "economic law" that was expected of him. In writing to J. N. A. Griswold, the chairman of the board, he began: "I can see no better way of fixing the pay of shopmen than on the general basis of supply and demand," and then added the defeating qualification, "bringing

[12] C. E. Perkins to T. J. Potter, August 13, 1885 (Archoives of Chicago, Burlington & Quincy Railroad, Newberry Library, Chicago, Illinois).
[13] R. Harris to J. M. Forbes, July 30, 1877 (Archives of Chicago, Burlington & Quincy Railroad, Newberry Library, Chicago, Illinois).
[14] R. Harris to C. E. Perkins, August 6, 1877 (Archives of Chicago, Burlington & Quincy Railroad, Newberry Libary, Chicago, Illinois).

to the subject, however, broad views, and not reducing pay to starvation wages simply because there may be in the market, for the time being, many men out of employment."[15] Similarly, in line with his general ideas of utilitarian social justice, Harris suggested a system of ninety-day notice in case of any change in pay. He presented this suggestion in terms of the adherence to "economic law" expected in his role: "The tendency of this would be," he argued, "that it would cause the men to feel that they were not so much under the arbitrary action of the officers of the Co. as they were under the inexorable laws of supply and demand."[16]

Still another example of Harris' urging deviant views in proper-role language was his desire to end Sunday train service. He assured the chairman that "it is not from a religious aspect that I propose to urge this, but entirely from an economic aspect, I am so sure of the value of Sunday rest to me that nothing could convince me that it would not be valuable to everyone. . . ."[17] It might be noted that for a number of reasons Harris was removed from the presidency about a year later.

But even Harris, the most obviously deviant of these executives, confined his unorthodoxy within relatively narrow limits. Among these sixty-one railroad leaders there were no strong believers in social democracy, religious zealots, open atheists, idealistic philosophers, artists, poets, or outstanding philanthropists. The politicians among them were routine and distinguished for little beyond able, hard-headed manipulation. Forbes might be classified as a scholar, although he did not so consider himself; and Henry Villard could, by broad definition, be called a literary man. But both were relatively orthodox in their political, social, and economic views. The uniformities illustrate not only the pressures of the role on participants, but also suggest

[15] R. Harris to J. N. A. Griswold, November 21, 1877 (Archives of Chicago, Burlington & Quincy Railroad, Newberry Library, Chicago, Illinois).
[16] R. Harris to J. N. A. Griswold, October 1, 1877 (Archives of Chicago, Burlington & Quincy Railroad, Newberry Library, Chicago, Illinois).
[17] R. Harris to J. N. A. Griswold, August 1, 1877 (Archives of Chicago, Burlington & Quincy Railroad, Newberry Libary, Chicago, Illinois).

the more or less unconscious use of role definition as a selective device for initially excluding the unorthodox.

Analysis of the thinking of other parts of the business community probably would bring out similar group uniformities. American culture may have mirrored its economic needs for utilitarian standardization. But it may also be true that corporate leaders, like politicians in power, felt the social and economic responsibilities of their position, as well as the uncertainties of tenure, and sought more than most men to conform to the expectations of their "constituents." Orthodox failure could be attributed to forces beyond the control of the entrepreneur, but unorthodoxy and failure was a deadly combination.

IV

Beyond any gains for the specialized student of business administration or railroading, how does a social role for the railroad executive, in so far as we have been able to define it, aid in the interpretation of American History? To begin with, it replaces inexact implications as to the character or motivation of railroad leaders that appear in the histories of this period with more definite hypotheses that do not depend upon dubious guesses about individual motives. While the role characteristics indicated in the case of the railroad executive may not reveal much that was not previously assumed, they provide an explanation for various attitudes and a scheme for their logical arrangement which can be elaborated and amended from additional evidence. Refusal to aid a young boy who had lost both legs in a railroad accident, for example, is seen not as unusual callousness on the part of the president of the Michigan Central, but as normal action in accordance with the sanctions of the social role regarding the conservation of the stockholders' money. Similarly, the strong sanctions for executive conduct in accord with the assumed laws of supply and demand explain much of what would seem today to be short-sighted personnel or labor policy.

Social role was an intangible control that operated within certain limits, not an exact prescription for every act. The particular interests of the small compact group on the board of directors set conceptions of the proper executive role somewhat different from those that arose from the experience of western managers surrounded with operating problems. This helps to explain the fact observed by Julius Grodinsky in his Iowa Pool study that the managers of roads which, on the basis of ownership interests, should have acted in harmony often battled over rates and traffic.[18] This also shows how new policies that might ultimately alter the role could rise from the bottom as well as come down from the top. In spite of occasional conflicts in role behavior, however, the relatively tight control of railroad affairs on a nation-wide basis by the attitudes of eastern financiers is a highly significant feature of American economic and social development. It explains, for instance, some of the mechanics of social control and cultural continuity that prevented frontier customs and behavior from being wholly products of their local environment. It also indicates the complexity of cultural change. Shifts in opinion regarding proper business practices in Dubuque, Iowa, might have to be transmitted from Boston financial circles. And, on the other hand, exploitation of new business opportunities on the upper Mississippi might be impeded by the fact that the social role of the railroad managers involved was not immediately responsive to local conditions.

By its very nature a uniform and well-understood role offers resistance to any change in conditions. And presumably the rigidity should be to some degree proportional to the precision of the role and the sanctioning force of the defining group. Thus a role set by a closed and conventional group in Boston could explain "cultural lag" not only in the West but in Boston itself. Rigidity of role definitions may be the chief difference between a "young" and an "old" civilization. The assumption that the executive roles in large corporations were particularly clear also serves to explain the widely held belief that big corporations are

[18] *The Iowa Pool* (Chicago: University of Chicago Press, 1950).

slower than small enterprises in adapting their policies to new conditions.

Ultimately, it seems possible that well-understood social roles will provide us with the needed concepts for relating factually verifiable sets of economic or social interests to concomitant ideas, attitudes, and patterns of behavior.

IX: Business and the
Democratic Tradition*

In the eyes of the rest of the world, America has been a "young" nation. A dynamic system of production and distribution has been an outstanding characteristic of its culture. In spite of well-defined corporate roles, American business is still regarded as a force leading to desirable change in society. But beyond this general belief relatively little attention has been given to just what part business actually has played and is playing in shaping American culture. For example, could Charles Wilson's unfortunate statement about the country and General Motors be properly rephrased as "What happens in General Motors is representative of American thought and action"?

The answer to that question should throw considerable light on two of the most important problems which baffle industrial leaders today: first, the negative reactions of so many Americans, reflected every day in newspapers, novels, public opinion surveys, and the like, to the values and objectives of industrial leaders; second, the resistance of peoples elsewhere in the world to the American way of life, in competition with the ideology of communism.

* Reprinted with permission from the *Harvard Business Review*, vol. 34, March-April 1956, pp. 39-48.

I

To suggest answers to the question of whether American business firms collectively are representative of the main elements of American culture, we must begin by considering some of the history of the interplay of business ideas and more general beliefs. The first half of the twentieth century has embraced such sweeping change in practically all areas of life that it is often difficult to decide what is basic and what is superficial, what is cause and what is effect. Nevertheless, we can identify some of the trends leading to the cultural relationships which prevail today.

Up to 1929 businessmen shared an increasing confidence in the future of America as they conceived it. While they had been under attack in the early part of the century from socialist groups and from progressives in both major parties, the criticism had spent itself and subsided. Meanwhile, business successfully weathered the panic of 1907, and was raised by war orders from the depression of 1914. "Back to normalcy" in 1920 meant to businessmen a return to the ideas of McKinley with the approval of the American people.

The very backbone of business thinking in "the good old days" was the idea of a self-regulating economy—an economy which, if left alone by government and other "non-economic" power groups such as labor unions, would always tend toward a position of equilibrium, where all the many day-to-day decisions made on the basis of immediate self-advantage would somehow have the cumulative effect of full employment and equitable distribution of income. This doctrine, taught in schools and colleges for many generations, was believed in by so many people outside the business group that it came to be in fact one of the major elements of American culture of that earlier period.

Prosperity after World War I, except for a short sharp depression in 1921, re-enforced the concept of the self-regulating economy. At the same time, new business ideas were emerging regarding the role of leadership in managing the system. Walter

Gifford, president of American Telephone & Telegraph, wrote in 1926:

New conditions have called a new type of man to lead the new kind of business organization. . . . These men must take a long view ahead. They cannot decide questions merely on the basis of immediate advantage, because their company is going to be in business long after they are dead.[1]

The basic contradiction between this idea of leadership and the concept of self-regulation was not immediately evident. The 1920's were a period of buoyant optimism and conservatism for business leaders, government administrators friendly to business helped to preserve the satisfaction with outworn ideas. The effects of a better financial system and big corporations were thought to have brought a new stability to economic life.

Faith in the future of the economy was bolstered by the belief which many intellectual leaders had in inevitable social evolution. Herbert Spencer's idea that Darwin's theory of biological advance through competitive struggle applied also to the social system was still in good standing. While beneficent evolution might be questioned by economists trained in the German tenet that "economic laws" depend on the social aims of the system involved or in the American philosophy of William James and John Dewey that truth is what works, these doubters appear to have been a small minority. As for the businessman, social Darwinism was simply another way of stating the "law of nature" that assured success to an able, hard-working man in a competitive society.

The evolutionary idea readily lent itself to elaboration in a doctrine of a national elite of successful businessmen. From a study of statements of men speaking for the National Association of Manufacturers and the U.S. Chamber of Commerce in the 1920's, James W. Prothero has worked out six interrelated articles of belief:

[1] *World's Work,* June 1926, quoted from Hermann Krooss, "Business Opinion Between Two Wars," unpublished Ph.D. thesis, New York University, 1947, p. 22.

(1) The business elite are superior to other men in ability.
(2) The test of ability is competitive earnings.
(3) Material or economic progress is the important goal.
(4) Social stability is necessary.
(5) Popular or majority control is dangerous.
(6) Individualism must be preserved.[2]

Granted that these views were expressed by the level of businessmen chosen to head a then inactive National Association of Manufacturers and a Chamber of Commerce that faced few issues, yet they do indicate a tendency present in other business thought in this decade of great confidence. They also represent the continuing dilemma of business—standing for technological and scientific advance at the same time it wants social and political conservatism.

But the business ideas of "the good old days" were to meet severe opposition. And the cause was not so much social and political change outside of business as the failure to maintain material or economic progress on the part of business itself.

While the late 1920's had produced increasingly high income for the top tenth of the population, there were no important gains for the lower income groups and no rate of real capital formation that could insure against collapse and stagnation. Fundamentally, America's businessmen, lulled by confidence in automatic economic adjustment, were running an industrial machine whose intricacies they did not understand. As a matter of fact, neither businessmen themselves nor the government administrators and economists had any real appreciation of such crucial economic relationships as those between worker morale and productivity, government spending and consumer demand, private saving and stimulation of investment, administered prices and economic rigidity. Business soon learned the precariousness of its new cultural position through bitter experience. Popular confidence in the satisfactory progress of a self-regulating economy was broken in the depression of the 1930's—and the Darwinian philosophical defense had been modi-

[2] James W. Prothero, *The Dollar Decade: Business Ideas in the 1920's* (Baton Rouge: Louisiana State University Press, 1954), pp. 209, 210.

fied by a biological theory of mutation, or inexplicable alterations rather than gradual evolution by the competitive process.

To many Americans it appeared that with the frontier gone
and with a "mature" industrial plant the economy would stag-
nate unless government provided new incentives and opportunities. Capitalism appeared to have lost its dynamics; a higher
and higher standard of living no longer seemed assured as the
automatic result of the quest for personal wealth. With a declining birth rate, Robert E. Wood, chairman of the board of
Sears Roebuck, warned:

> A decline in population must inevitably result in a lower rather
> than higher standard of living . . . . the sun has passed its zenith and
> the shadows of afternoon have begun to fall.[3]

It may be hard for younger men of the 1960's to realize the
degree to which business confidence and prestige were shaken by
the events of 1931 to 1933. As a result business leaders lacked
morale to oppose the idea that the government aid to business
offered by the Hoover Administration was necessary, or the subsequent idea, reluctantly accepted even by its political advocates
at the time, that government must assume responsibility for the
economic welfare and security of its citizens. A radically new
conception of the use of federal power was beginning to develop, implying not only relief and social security, but also
government investment and subsidy to stimulate purchasing
power and employment.

Not that businessmen as a whole agreed with these views;
they blamed the depression either on the upsetting effects of
World War I or on the frailty of individuals, and criticized the
spending policies of Congress in the Hoover Administration. In
1932, for example, Alfred P. Sloan, Jr., president of General
Motors, said: "The trouble at Washington is that large sums
have been voted for post offices, pensions and bonuses not justified."[4]

By the mid-1930's many businessmen were saying that govern-

[3] Quoted from Hermann Krooss, *op. cit.,* p. 149.
[4] *The New York Times,* June 7, 1932, quoted from Hermann Krooss, *op.
cit.,* p. 121.

ment had already intruded so far that the economy was no longer self-regulating. Possibly, they conceded, the new economy, because it was a mixture of government and private enterprise, needed certain government incentives to avoid the danger of stagnation; but the more state aid it received, the more mixed it tended to become and hence the more aid it would need in the future—and so on and on until the private sector might vanish altogether. Thus did businessmen get caught in the dilemma which to this day they have not been able to resolve completely.

Loss of confidence in the theory of self-regulation was bound to lead to a reassessment of business ideas and new conceptions of the place of business in American society. This painful struggle for readjustment must be seen in relation to another major change in society, the rise of bureaucracy.

Judged by the standards of 1800, American society in 1900 was already bureaucratic, but apparently this fact did not attract much attention at the time. Congressional debates and serious writing were concerned with the struggles of little business against big business and of individuals against the "laws of nature," but not with the struggle of individuals against collective bureaucracy. Not until the rise of collectivist governments of both right and left in Europe after 1917 were Americans alerted to this issue. The further growth of enormous business companies in the 1920's led intellectuals to extend the scope of their questioning, and the New Deal at last made bureaucracy a major concern.

Although the growth of big government first called general attention to it, the bureaucratic system was actually a response to industrial mass production. Big plants required big management, and the social and economic problems growing from concentration of working population necessitated more and more govenment. Since the company big enough to have a true bureaucracy—that is, a broad layer of middle management which neither initiated policies nor directly carried them out—would normally be run by professional executives, the rise of bureaucracy also went hand in hand with that of managerial enterprises.

II

By mid-century a large part of the individual's contacts were with representatives of various large organizations. Social scientists and artists tended increasingly to see both government and business bureaucracy as parts of the larger problem of the individual in a highly organized impersonal society. Writers such as Frederic Wakeman (*The Hucksters*) and John P. Marquand (*Point of No Return*) turned out penetrating satires of the business bureaucracy with the implicit admonition that the individual should rebel and find some way of asserting his right to a unique human role.

Just as Americans in general had long cherished an image of the individual on the model of the independent, courageous, self-reliant frontiersman, business philosophy in particular had dwelt upon the ruggedly individualistic element in the American national character. It was the existence of thousands of these centers of independent enterprise that made the self-regulating economy work. But with the depression, the resultant increase in government supervision and regulation, and the concurrent growth of organizational complexity in corporations, the individual seemed to account for less and less. People still clung to the idea of the importance of the individual, but it was not clear how the concept was being supported in practice.

Business leaders did not usually see their own companies, with their hierarchical bureaucracies, welfare policies, and demands for loyalty, as playing a part in the constriction of individualism. But there were others who could recognize a new order. Thus, *Life* editor John K. Jessup pointed out: "For economic purposes the organization is more important than what it owns, or who works for it. It has a life of its own. It began as a mere legal person. It has acquired a social personality."[5] Management's devotion to the welfare of the corporate unit necessarily emphasized loyalty, trusteeship, self-sacrificing service, planning, and security, and de-emphasized personal eccentricity and individual

[5] John K. Jessup, "A Political Role for the Corporation," *Fortune*, August, 1952, p. 113.

acquisitiqn. This shift in emphasis in the society was gradual, as with all cultural change, and was in an early stage by 1960.

Whether one looked at government as did most business leaders when they lamented the loss of concern for the individual, or at big business as did novelists and some small businessmen, the conclusion was inescapable that individualism, as traditionally conceived, was declining. Fewer men were left in impersonal relations to markets where their personal eccentricities did not count, and where individual cleverness might win immediate cash rewards. More men had to try to please their organizational associates by some degree of conformity. Businessmen were voluntarily surrendering individual freedom in order to get ahead in a bureaucratic society.

While the traditional business beliefs in individualism, competitive survival, and freedom from governmental interference were being undermined, the social prestige of great wealth was also declining under the influences of mass production and the managerial system. Luxury articles became increasingly standardized and within reach of most consumers. As late as 1930 a Ford and a Lincoln represented vastly different levels of motoring pleasure and appearance, but by 1960 many people could not tell which was which. The large house, in 1900 the chief symbol of wealth, was becoming rare; there was no longer a depressed immigrant or agricultural labor group to provide cheap servants and the mobility of corporate executives was such that they hesitated to invest more in any one location than could easily be recovered through a sale. Sociologist David Riesman wrote on the new trend of the upper-income group toward "inconspicuous consumption."[6]

Re-enforcing these trends was the increasing equality of income after taxes. Taxes appeared destined to remain high and to be progressive against larger incomes on both the state and national levels. Aside from preparation for war, the industrial system needed streets, highways, schools, colleges, hospitals, and other collective facilities on a scale never thought of by earlier

---

[6] David Riesman, *From Conspicuous Consumption to Conspicuous Production* (Glencoe, Ill.: The Free Press, 1954) , pp. 224-225.

generations, and most of the money had to come from taxes. During the nearly continuous boom from 1940 on, elastic business expense accounts and tax savings on capital gains did encourage a good deal of lavish consumption, but by the standards of earlier days the rich were heavily taxed.

In the field of social welfare and philanthropy, bureaucratic action was superseding the individual decisions of successful businessmen. Since the government allowed corporations to contribute a part of their income to charitable or educational institutions before paying taxes, there was a large saving in having such gifts made directly by the companies rather than by the receivers of already taxed dividends. This led to the setting up of general foundations such as The Ford Foundation, and to direct corporate support of higher education. Explaining his participation in this movement, Chairman Frank W. Abrams of the Standard Oil Company of New Jersey said:

I know I can't take any credit for this. I'm just an ordinary business guy that got shoved into something. It's like being thrown into a Billy Sunday meeting, I suppose, and getting converted. You didn't want to go in, but somebody pushed you—they thought you needed it. And it has been rather overwhelming, and highly satisfying.[7]

The importance of this shift is probably not in its influence on the character of education or welfare agencies. It may be easy to imagine that higher education, perhaps the most influential conditioner of the political and social ideas of future leaders, will fall under the control of business, and a few businessmen have added to these fears by writing of the obligation of the colleges to teach the free-enterprise system. However, private education has always been supported by men who have made their money in business. Donors seem no more likely to interfere with academic freedom as corporate executives than they did as private citizens.

The real significance of corporate giving is the way it marks the emergence of the big company as a quasi-public institution with social and political responsibilities. But while this can be

[7] A. R. Raskin, "The Corporation on the Campus," *The New York Times Magazine,* April 17, 1955, p. 63.

interpreted as a fresh source of democracy to counteract the increased influence of centralized government, it is a very impersonal kind of democracy—it is the democracy of big units rather
than the democracy of individuals.

III

There still exists the problem that has beset the corporate
form of organization since its beginnings in the early nineteenth
century—the inability to achieve a democratic system of operation within the company.

The spirit of business has always been the efficient exercise of
authority from the top down. But business is the leading institution in a social system called democracy; to be truly representative it too must be democratic. And democracy works from the
bottom up. This means more than equality of opportunity for
those qualified to rise, more than democratic manners that allow
a worker to call the president by his first name. It means policy
formation on a participative basis and an increased business
willingness to study and respond to the problems and values of
American society. As Sir George Schuster, a British business
leader, put it:

If we try, as many of us do who hold managerial responsibilities, to
set out a list of ideals which we are to aim at, or which we think are
good for people for whose employment we are responsible, then I
think we are doomed to disaster. We have to work *with* an intelligent
population.[8]

One unmistakable clash between the democratic and the business traditions has been the old assumption that workers are
purely "economic men," interested only in material satisfactions.
This assumption came under attack as a result of Elton Mayo's
study at the Hawthorne plant of Western Electric in the late

---

[8] Eugene Staley, Editor, *Creating an Industrial Civilization: A Report of
the Corning Conference* (New York: Harper & Brothers, 1952), pp. 204-205,
italics added.

1920's, and his book, *The Human Problems of an Industrial Civilization*.[9] But the results of this advanced thinking have been slow to spread, and there has been a tendency to apply so-called "human relations" formulas as gimmicks or manipulative devices rather than sincerely seeking participation.

As late as 1952 *Time* ran a special two-page section, "Human Relations: A New Art Brings a Revolution in Industry." One of the illustrative cases concerned a change in the method of pajama making:

One group was simply told of the change, another was told of the necessity for it and permitted to work out for itself the necessary revisions in quotas and rates. Result: the second group's production quickly passed the old average of 60 hourly units per worker, and reached more than 80. The first group barely exceeded 50 units, and 17 per cent of its members shortly quit.

The article ends with a quotation from Clarence Francis, chairman of the board of General Foods:

It is ironic that Americans—the most advanced people technically, mechanically and industrially—should have waited until a comparatively recent period to inquire into the most promising single source of productivity: namely the human will to work. It is hopeful on the other hand that the search is now underway.[10]

Despite many articles and books, since then, there still exists "a great demand for guidance and enlightenment on the part of . . . businessmen, who apparently feel all of a sudden that they are deficient in the practice of human relations."[11] Such a feeling of the need to do something in this area is evidence of the persistence of the problem as well as of some progress.

A weakness in the search for what creates the will to work is

[9] Boston, Division of Research, Harvard Business School, reprinted 1946. See also Loren Baritz, *The Servants of Power: A History of the Use of Social Science in American Industry* (Middletown, Conn.: Wesleyan University Press, 1960).

[10] *Time*, April 14, 1952, p. 97.

[11] Edward C. Bursk, "Introduction," *Human Relations for Management* (New York: Harper & Brothers, 1956), a collection of articles from the *Harvard Business Review*, 1950-1955.

failure to recognize the wholeness of human personality. The will to work depends not only on good working conditions and respect for the dignity of the worker, but also on the employee's approval of the company, its policies, and its roles in society. The talk of businessmen and labor leaders alike is still too much in terms of material wants and satisfactions. Eric Larabee, then an editor of *Harper's Magazine*, noted at the Corning Glass Works' conference of businessmen and scholars that there was a tendency on both sides to "speak of 'human values' as distinct entities, almost as though they had similar qualities to goods and services."[12]

Seldom does business discussion rise to the level of searching for new positive nonmaterial values that could make business a world-wide standard-bearer of democracy. The fact that the *Harvard Business Review*, which is read by top business executives, should have received a citation in 1955 from The Laymen's Movement for a Christian World for a series of five articles providing "insight concerning spiritual values in business,"[13] as if that were something unique, is simply a sign of the rarity of business thinking about the nonmaterial aspects of organization.

Lack of democracy is certainly not a failing peculiar to American business. On the contrary, American business is probably more democratic than business anywhere else in the world. The trouble is that in the course of its growth from small shop to great corporation it has failed to embody in its structure and operation some basic ideals of American culture.

Defining specific ideals in a complex culture like that of the United States is a difficult task, avoided by most scholars of a scientific bent, and done only impressionistically by visiting literary men or journalistic pundits. Such playing with abstractions is clearly not a game for active business leaders. Yet there have been some cultural common denominators which few Americans would question; they find expression in sayings and beliefs passed on to children by generations of parents and reinforced by repetition in millions of schoolbooks.

---

[12] Eugene Staley, *op. cit.*, p. 204.
[13] *Harvard Business Review*, v. 34 (March-April 1956), p. 136.

Some of these, such as the belief that rational effort counts, that change is generally good, that active mastery of a problem rather than fatalistic acceptance is the American way, or that interest in the external world of things is better than inner contemplation, have reinforced the attitudes of businessmen. But other themes that emphasize the American democratic and religious heritage, such as the need for justification of behavior in terms of Christian morality, the strong belief in equality as a law of nature or the "cult of the common man," and the right of every adult male to have an equal voice in making decisions affecting the common welfare, have often conflicted with business action.[14] These latter are basic ideals, however, that underlie the operation of most social organizations, of almost all Protestant religions, and of all American governments.

The average businessman, whether of 1860 or 1960, would probably subscribe to these latter ideals in principle, but he would admit, when pressed on the subject, that often they do not appear immediately applicable in business. Business he might argue, has to have a system of ideals of its own, such as physical efficiency, substantial rewards for unusual ability, and clear lines of authority based on the sanction of ownership. Insofar as the coexistence of these two systems is reconcilable, it is on the basis that business is a special part of the nation's activity which justifies its deviations from the precepts of the Bible and the Declaration of Independence by a flood of products that make a better life possible in all other spheres. From the sacrifice of certain ideals on the economic altar comes their richer fulfillment in the life of the nation.

This rift between business ideals and those of the common people helps to explain the ambiguous popular attitude toward

[14] These values or beliefs have been suggested by the analyses of anthropologists and sociologists. While no formal consensus has been attempted, I have never come across basic opposition to the formulations given here. See Clyde Kluckhohn, *Mirror for Man: The Relation of Anthropology to Modern Life* (New York: Whittlesey House, 1949), p. 232; Robin W. Williams, Jr., *American Society: A Sociological Interpretation* (New York: Alfred A. Knopf, Inc., 1951), pp. 441-442; and F. L. K. Hsu, "Cultural Factors," *Factors in Economic Development: Principles and Patterns*, edited by H. F. Williamson and John A. Buttrick (New York: Prentice-Hall, Inc., 1954), pp. 340-41.

business leaders. They are respected for their material success, their control over jobs, and their ability to supply capital or credit, but regarded as lacking in the moral and spiritual qualities desired in the top level of national leaders. In American folklore the farmer's values and attitudes are virtues, while those of the businessman foster such vices as covetousness and vanity. The upbringing of the poor country boy was idealized and regarded as a guarantee that, even if he later achieved economic success, his basic ideas would be moral in the Protestant religious sense, and they would be democratic in the common people's sense.

Businessmen are seriously troubled by public distrust only when it takes the form of regulatory legislation. The almost unchallenged position of business executives as decision makers in their own sphere of action over many generations gives them the feeling that their ideas are right and that the public should conform to them. Businessmen tend to regard other types of leaders as unreliable or incompetent. The motives of politicians are suspect as corrupt and insincere. Professors, ministers, and literary men are held to be impractical and likely to have theories dangerous to social stability.

This anti-intellectual attitude has been strong since, at least, the mid-nineteenth century. Merle E. Curti notes that "American respect for business, and the businessman's inadequate appreciation of the intellectual have, by tradition, been pretty generally taken for granted."[15] Thus the businessman has been able to a degree to live in his part of the culture by his own precepts, regarding other beliefs as unimportant to the main task at hand, profit from the material improvement of the nation.

That the tacit assumption of superior business understanding still persists is illustrated by an interesting example. In 1950 Edward Bernays, one of the most prescient and philosophical of public relations men, promoter of the concept that public rela-

[15] Merle E. Curti, "Intellectuals and Other People," *The American Historical Review*, January 1955, p. 265. See also Richard Hofstadter, *Anti-Intellectualism in American Life* (New York: Alfred A. Knopf, 1963).

tions was a two-way street down which ideas came from the public to business, nevertheless delivered a speech in Boston on "How American Business Can Sell the American Way of Life to the American People."[16] One wonders if a small voice at the other end of the two-way street replied: "How Can the American People Sell the American Way of Life to Business?"

Actually, this instance is somewhat unfair to both Bernays and to advanced business thought, but it illustrates the unfortunate if more or less unconscious historic assumption that society should conform to what managers deem best for business.

Often serving as the justification for business dogmatism has been the idea that business decisions are squarely based on the requirements of the market. No doubt in the old days of small business, low mechanization, and weak market controls the businessman struggling for survival in a competitive situation had little leeway. But the big companies of today, the ones that set the tone of business thinking, do have considerable control over prices in the market. And, as already noted, such companies have already gone far in the support of community services, education, and welfare plans for workers.

The fact remains that the decisions to do these good deeds have not generally been participated in by their beneficiaries. Aside from dealings with organized labor, there are few democratic procedures in business by which opinion from below can effectively influence the major actions of those on top, or by which changes in policy can be opened to advanced discussions. The practical difficulties in the way are great, though not as great as they once were. But if business is to be truly democratic, then the challenge is to find some way to overcome them.

IV

The challenge is all the greater because of the effect upon the rest of the world. In the past the heterogeneous, loosely knit institutions and organizations constituting business never faced

[16] Edward Bernays, *Public Relations* (Norman: University of Oklahoma Press, 1949), p. 336.

the need for a "theology" that would sell the faith to the rest of the world. Now there is an extra reason for business to emphasize qualities that have always been presumed to lie outside its its immediate concerns. That this is asking a great deal of business is obvious, but the importance is obvious too.

The aftermath of World War II has placed the American business system in an international spotlight. The United States emerged in the late 1940's as the only Western nation strong enough to undertake world leadership, and she led from a position of strength based primarily on the success of her economic system. Thus, for better or for worse, American business has become a key protagonist in the physical struggle with world communism.

However, the contest is not only a matter of material superiority, and the fight for world influence cannot be won by economic means alone. If such were the case, America would triumph, and American businessmen, as the directors of these economic forces, would be the world's natural leaders. But the United States is battling for men's minds—their hopes, aims, and allegiance—and it is increasingly evident that success depends on a spiritual and intellectual appeal rather than on mere respect for economic power. Approval must be voluntary and cannot be commanded. And although America has had little difficulty selling the products of her fields and factories overseas—her industrial machinery, agricultural implements, petroleum products, grain and crude cotton, automotive equipment—she has not yet sold the rest of the world on the soundness of the American experience.

Because the contacts of the mass of the people with things American are to such a large extent with businessmen and their products, the representatives of United States economic power must assume a significant role in this winning of social approval. Thus the very success of American business has placed it in a position for which it never consciously prepared, and for which it is not especially fitted.

It is significant that industry, whose strength so largely gave rise to the idea of American world mission, found its traditional policies thrown into confusion when the need for action developed. Business was swept progressively into a new military order of subsidies to foreign nations, massive government investment, stockpiling of scarce materials, and armament manufacture. Should executives resist the advance of peacetime government foreign aid and arms expenditures at the risk of turning the world over to fascism or communism, or should they accept the administration program at the risk of never again being free from the need of government aid? For a hundred years American private enterprise had prepared its defense against socialist revolution, but, it had given little thought to the danger of simply being absorbed by a "capitalist" state.

True choice has scarcely been possible since cooperation with government is the road to profits for the stockholders, and such is the traditional aim of management. For those companies with government contracts, and this includes most of the giants, it is clearly advantageous to cultivate close relations with government officials, particularly in the defense department. For this purpose retired generals, admirals, and high-level civilian officials have made valuable business executives. While quantitatively this movement is small, it does raise fears in some minds of a union of undemocratic forces in business and government—this at a time when the need seems to be for business to give assurances in the opposite direction.

The challenge to business to play its necessary role in American intellectual and spiritual world leadership is far more difficult to meet than the adjustment to government contracting. In the confident days of 1900, evolution, Christianity, the Anglo-Saxon character, and the virtues of democracy appeared to promise the eventual world supremacy of the American way. But now the struggle for supremacy is no longer some unforeseeable situation of the future. And much of the spiritual equipment counted on in 1900 is relatively ineffective. The ways of evolution have become a mystery; conventional Christianity, while strong at home, seems a weak weapon against communism; the strength of Anglo-Saxon character no longer controls the people of backward areas; and the political institutions of the

Anglo-American tradition are easily misunderstood and often not immediately applicable to people differently trained.

The one aspect of American life that the whole world continues to respect is its material success. Indeed, the results accruing from the American business system are the strongest arguments the United States and her allies hold in the contest for world allegiance. If the rest of the world could be shown that our business principles are an integral part of a larger value system beneficial to them and possible of adoption, they might be won over.

Our business system cannot be transplanted complete and full-grown on other cultures, any more than our political order, our legal and ethical codes, or our moral precepts and beliefs, could be. But there is an essence of equalitarian liberalism in our social, political, and economic way of life which can be transmitted. The task of the businessman in contact with foreigners is to recognize that in other cultures this essence may take new governmental and economic forms and to tolerate them if they are in the spirit of the best in our total way of life.

V

The chronicle of the changes in business ideology since 1900 make future adjustment seem possible. Business has modified its ideas and adapted itself to the inevitable changes in the social and political complexion of the country. Granted that the adjustments were often made grudgingly, and sometimes incompletely, yet they were made. From a philosophy of the self-regulating economy presided over by an elite group who could take care of themselves and who had no responsibility for the welfare of others, businessmen as a whole have come to a realization that bigness necessitates certain government controls over the economy; they accept the fact that with their position of great influence in the nation must go some accountability for the general well-being.

Nevertheless, business is far from ready to assume the missionary task which has been thrust on it. It must certainly work at making its own internal operations reflect more adequately the democratic ideals we want to communicate abroad. A more basic problem, perhaps—the same one which confronts all other segments of American society—is the need for reanalysis and rearticulation of the ideals and values we want the rest of the world to accept.

In spite of the widely held view that the United States is a "business society," the great majority of the people who work for salaries or wages do not regard themselves as businessmen. Regardless of prosperity, better public relations, and more independent business enterprisers in relation to the rest of the population, a feeling of unity with the aims of business leadership is lacking. People apparently respect but do not trust business leaders. Corporations may in truth be becoming guardians of the common welfare, but the public is not yet convinced. In May 1949, according to a Roper poll:

A majority of the people . . . believe that very few businessmen have the good of the nation in mind when they make their important decisions. . . . They think, therefore, that government should keep a sharp eye on business.[17]

American businessmen, for all their important position in society today, do not epitomize America as did the independent farmers of an earlier era. Perhaps, capitalist business cannot by its nature succeed in an attempt to mirror the value structure of the society. Yet that does not lessen the need for clarification of the various traditions and beliefs which America desires to communicate to the rest of the world. Philosophers and anthropologists point to the confusion and conflict in American values resulting partly from business practice; religious leaders question especially some of business' ethical precepts, asking

[17] *Fortune,* May 1949; see also Elmo Roper, "The Public Looks at Business," *Harvard Business Review,* v. 27, p. 165.

"whether the secular functions of society, each existing of itself and for itself, can be relied on to serve human destiny."[18]

If the "image of America" has failed to win the unreserved approval and support of the people of the rest of the world, it is partly because we ourselves are not quite clear in our minds what America does and should represent—no wonder that foreigners are so often confused and uncertain about the American way.[19] Businessmen—and other representatives of our nation— have tried to talk in terms of democracy, individualism, inalienable rights, opportunity for all, and so forth; these concepts are, unfortunately, merely words and will never serve to unite the world around American leadership until they are given validity, until we are sure what we mean by them, and until the facts of American culture are aligned with our ideas about it.

Much of the conflict, much of the apparent lack of unity and purpose in our national life, comes from our failure so far to reconcile business attitudes and aims—such as the pursuit of an ever higher standard of living—with the other fundamental values stemming from American religious and democratic traditions. If business could look at itself, analyze its values, and try to realign them with those broader ideals of the good society, it could help more than any other force in the country to make stronger and more valid America's message to an uncertain world.

At the stage of technology now present in the United States, greater productivity results from treating the employee as a human being who should be attached to his work by intellectual approval and a sense of "belonging" at the job as well as by the need of the pay check. The management that adopts the gospel of the democratic custodianship of economic opportunity is going to have improved morale from top to bottom.

Big business, as we have seen, is beginning to move in this direction. Small and medium-size business is still highly com-

[18] Marquis W. Childs and Douglas Cater, *Ethics in a Business Society* (New York: New American Library of World's Literature, 1954), p. 176.
[19] See Max Ascoli, "The Hidden America," *The Reporter*, December 1, 1955, p. 11.

petitive, is often inadequately financed, and has less leeway to take non-material considerations into account; here progress will probably be a matter not of years but of decades. From the standpoint of public relations at home, this is discouraging, since most Americans work for small or medium-size business. The image of our society presented abroad, however, may change more rapidly. Almost all foreign contacts are—with the agencies or products of sizable American companies—organizations that are large enough at least to be conscious of their place in a new business order and to be capable of providing leadership in that direction if they want to.

To hope for moral or spiritual inspiration from any size of business is asking for new functions from an institution originally designed to supply only material wants. But the modern corporation has inevitably become more than an economic institution, and its managers have more than material responsibilities. In the words of Meyer Kestenbaum, president of Hart, Shaffner and Marx:

We need now some people to tell us how to convert industrialism, which has great power, into the force for good in our own country and elsewhere that it can be. If we meet that challenge. I will say again that we are on the verge of a golden age.[20]

---

[20] Eugene Staley, *op. cit.*, p. 174.

X: The Continuing Challenge

In the preceding chapters the argument that the inner revolution calls for a new scientific study of history, and the elaboration of some of the elements in such an approach have been illustrated mainly by application to the institutions of business. In closing I wish to emphasize some general concepts underlying social science method and their challenge to new research by historians in all fields.

Scholars may rise to this challenge not only from aroused interest but also from necessity. The flood of scholarly historical writing during the last generation has made it increasingly hard to find projects of a conventional type that promise important new information. Like the American economy, history is on a high plateau of achievement from which the next steps onward and upward probably require departures from past practice. The easy paths have been followed, those that remain unexplored must be hard to discern or they would already have been pursued.

Physical scientists in similar situations have resumed their advance by creating new theories or hypotheses and by reworking existing data in new ways. While recognizing the stimulating effect that pure theory has had in social disciplines such as economics, it seems that the historian is more likely to progress by the second course. Specifically, I suggest, first, that more attention be given to published materials relating to certain basic institutions such as child-rearing, education, religion and ways of making a living; second, that classificatory methods be applied to materials now regarded as essentially qualitative; and third, that the reverse of this process be employed to derive new interpretive meaning from quantitative data. Or in other words, more effort to quantify the qualitative and vice versa. In addition, the significance of such findings can be greatly enhanced by comparison with the history of similar institutions or processes in other cultures.

Turning to the first type of suggestion for moving beyond the present plateau, more general use can be made of materials normally regarded as falling outside the main fields of historical interest. In spite of protests by three generations of historians, there is still a strong bias toward over-concentration on events connected with national politics; drama, ease of composition and the broadening sphere of governmental influence have kept national political history in its traditional place. It is still accepted as general history, whereas family, educational, religious or business history, as well as the history of the states, are regarded as special. New approaches and new tasks will arise merely from seeing the history of all the major social institutions as essential and closely interrelated. As a problem in historical synthesis, this means that the major focus should alter from period to period to emphasize the institutions in which change seems most important. National politics may occupy the center of the stage in one period, but give way to religion, education or business at other times.

Those institutions directly connected with the transmission of the culture from one generation to the next are particularly important. This has been impressed upon students of economic development through their quest for the causes of retarded material growth in cultures strikingly different from those of Western Europe and the United States. The findings have emphasized the basic importance of personality differences stemming from different family and educational conditioning. In the United States there is a large literature, stretching from Colonial times to the present, of advice to parents on the upbringing of children. As Bernard Bailyn has shown for the Colonial period, there is an even larger literature on American education. And there are further discussions of both child-rearing and education in political speeches, legislative debates, collections of sermons, autobiographies, and observations by foreign visitors. In all, there are great possibilities for better understanding of the development of American national character, types of personality, social structure and economic growth.

Such factors usually change very slowly. For most periods of American history they appear to be unaltered continuities. The historian, focussing on change and events, may easily slight their importance in the total situation. For example, parental attitudes regarding the value of time, the need for personal success, the existence of divine and natural laws appear to be fairly constant from the earliest settlements to, at least, the late nineteenth century. Being for any intervening period a part of the "given" culture, there has been a tendency not to waste time in trying to weight or type the elements in such continuity. Only in the early twentieth century when the impact of scientific ideas of psychology, child-rearing, and education produced middle and upper-class generations with different conditioning, was the importance of the old continuities clear.

One moral of this illustration is that it often requires a change to show the importance of continuities. Another, is that what appear to be unchanging continuities may not be in fact. Changes may be taking place in ways not directly reflected in any of the conventional indexes or in events. These alterations lead subtly to new situations and new resolutions of these situations. The Great Depression of the 1930's, for example, illustrated how far the real facts of economic relationships had departed from the old ideas regarding the self-regulating economy, without the change being perceived by more than a handful of observers.

The general historian obviously cannot continually be analyzing the character of continuities or subtle changes in every major institution, but he can keep as close a watch on areas basic to cultural change such as child-rearing, schooling, religious beliefs, and the institutions connected with making a living and accumulating economic power, as he does on problems of government.

Concentration on such gradual institutional change is methodologically more demanding than the verification and ordering of events. The abstract character of the concept of an institution is in itself a source of difficulty. From the standpoint of definition the term "institution" offers no more than the usual semantic problems. Sociologists find three characteristics inherent in institutions: first, organized social groups such as families or political parties; second, complex behavior patterns such as marriage, or competition in markets; and third, physical complexes such as churches, homes or factories.[1] It seems unlikely that many historians would disagree with this usage. Some sociologists also stress that institutions are built around values that are supported by prescribed norms of conduct.[2] In addition, institutions are almost infinitely divisible into sub-institutions. Government as a whole is an institution, but so is a bi-cameral legislature, the office of the President, or the conduct of elections.

Difficulties arise, not so much in agreeing upon the characteristics of an institution, but in finding ways of measuring or dividing indices of inter-institutional trends and pressures. This is particularly true of institutions such as the family, religion or business whose influences pervade the whole society. Take, for example, a specific instance from the history of business. By 1690 a large number of ministers were preaching sermons against contracting debts that could not be paid. At the same time, collecting domestic accounts was the major problem of the chief businessmen of the day, the importing merchants. Since avoidance of debt has not generally been a major emphasis of sermons the circumstantial case for business influence on religion seems good, but so far there is no reliable index or data that can be offered as direct evidence. In fact, business-like speech, thought and action were so general in American culture from the earliest days that they were accepted as normal and aroused

[1] Robert C. Hanson, "Institutions" in *Contemporary Society*, Joseph S. Roucek, ed., (New York: Philosophical Library, 1958), p. 65.
[2] Robin M. Williams, *American Society* (New York: Alfred A. Knopf, 1962), p. 31.

no comments. But working from circumstantial inference is a necessary road to new historical ideas, and searching for more evidence to support tentative conclusions is one of the chief sources of historical growth.

My second suggestion for progress in historiography is through efforts to classify, rank or otherwise systematize what is often regarded as unique or, at least, unmeasurable qualitative material. Rank orders, classifications to establish modes, norms or types all lead toward statements having quantitative significance. Samuel Hays, for example, has developed a number of correlations between shifts in voting behavior and changing socio-economic characteristics of Michigan counties by ranking them in order of the change between Republican and Democratic votes in two presidential elections. He has applied scalograms to legislative voting to establish significant correlations such as that between legislators who voted against prohibition measures and the religious affiliation of their constituents.

Many norms or types may be established without using any elaborate new methods. The normal characteristics of American cities of various sizes in 1850, for example, can be derived from the census, city directories, and urban histories. Such a classification may in turn result in new ideas regarding urbanization and suggest new lines of research. Similarly, one might establish the normal or modal characteristics of particular types of farms. By never erecting any framework of norms or measurement we leave ourselves open to being misled by a few instances and developing myths such as those about the prevalence of the self-made man among the leaders of business, or the economic importance of the civil war.

More than is generally realized, small numbers of cases are susceptible to mathematical tests for correlation. Using autobiographical data in relation to accepted theories of child psychology, Murray G. Murphey, for example, has made a mathematically strong case for correlation between early nineteenth century American child-rearing practices and a normally aggressive response by adult males to situations of threat. While one may say that his particular research merely gives systematic support to existing ideas, it presents a striking example of the quantification of qualitative materials by the use of mathematical logic.

Advances in the ordering or weighting of qualitative materials will also call attention to the need for new types of historical information. If, for example, one imagines, a little beyond the currently possible, to a time when we can quantify more aspects of power, personality, or incentive, it is highly probable that data will be needed that is not now being collected.

My third suggestion is for more consideration of what may be learned from analysis of quantitative series. While an army of economists and sociologists are collecting time series, only the historian is properly equipped to examine the full, interpretive meaning. Challenging to such research are the implications of American migration.

High spatial moblity may well be the most important cultural differential between American and European development. It may account for both the characteristics that Turner ascribed to the frontier and for many other features of American social economic and political development. Demographers are still working on a detailed record of inter-county migration, which on a nation-wide scale requires a massive expenditure of time. While the decadal figures on interstate migration indicate high levels, they undoubtedly fall short of the total of year to year, county to county, movements.[3]

Migrant groups have the measurable characteristics of including more young adult males than the average of the population. From this, plus uniform elements in the conditions of resettlement, a number of probable characteristics follow. The force of kinship relations lessens, migrants can seldom carry with them ascribed status, they are forced to succeed by their own efforts in a new environment, to do this they need to emphasize equality of opportunity, tolerance for the ways of others, cooperation

[3] See Everett S. Lee, Ann Ratner Miller, Carol P. Brainerd and Richard A. Easterlin, *Population Redistribution and Economic Growth in the United States 1870-1950*, vol. I (Philadelphia: American Philosophical Society) pp. 10-14.

and conformity, within reason, to local customs.[4] These are essentially the characteristics Turner attributed to the frontier, and in that area the two approaches coincide. But from 1850 on the most important areas of in-migration show the reverse of the above characteristics. There is for example a positive correlation between states that have small in-migration and conservatism in voting behavior.

Spatial restlessness may be connected with or may produce certain types of personality. As seen in Chapter II from 1910 to 1950 the rapidity of movement into and out of an old settled eastern community like Norristown, Pennsylvania, is very striking. From 1940 to 1950 the total number of residents remained practically unchanged, yet 37 per cent of the population moved out during the decade and 40 per cent moved in. This milling of the population was not a random motion. "The high in- and out-migration rates of each decade were largely attributable to the movement of repeated migrants into and out of the community . . . there was a large segment of the population which, through its continuous residence in Norristown, provided continuity and stability to the community."[5]

This study, therefore, suggests that many Americans have fallen into one of two types, those who continuously migrated and those who steadily stayed home. Regardless of any personality differences the first group were obviously spreaders of uniform cultural characteristics, while the latter conserved regional peculiarities. But it may well be that there are modal personality differences between the people who are urged to move and those who prefer to stay put; that the atmosphere of a new community may depend not only on the necessary attributes of migrants and the needs of a pioneer society, but also upon the predominance in its population of a migrant type.

The cultural characteristics that may depend either on the selective and conditioning aspects of migration or on the migrant type of personality are a challenge to the fertility of

[4] See Everett S. Lee, "The Turner Thesis Reexamined," *American Quarterly*, v. XIII, Spring 1961, pp. 77-83.

[5] Sidney Goldstein, *The Norristown Study*, (Philadelphia: University of Pennsylvania Press, 1961), p. 90.

imagination. In addition to those allied to the Turner concepts, there are other sets that have to do with all the major social institutions. Using business as an illustration, the ease with which Americans moved from one activity to another, from business to farming, or vice versa, the relatively good treatment of labor, the ease of democratic cooperation in big organizations may all be products of the conditioning effects of continuous migration. Thus the migration approach, resting basically on quantitative data, can explain qualitative aspects of American culture by a continuing general process, rather than by the conditioning force of a moving fringe area such as the frontier.

The illuminating force of comparative study is particularly obvious in relation to migration. England, for example, offers areas of in-migration, out-migration and high stability which can be matched against their counterparts in the United States. Research of this type emphasizes the danger in attributing too much to the uniqueness of American environment and too little to the effects of institutions and processes common to much of Western European culture.

The suggestions made in this chapter are the essence of what has been urged and illustrated throughout the book. The undermining of the traditional values of American and Western European culture in the twentieth century, the inner revolution, has placed an added burden on history. Now it should not only record the achievements of the past, but also try to find analogies applicable to a confused present. For this latter purpose, historians should examine more systematically the institutions basic to cultural continuity or change, should look more searchingly for order or structure in trends generally treated as qualitative, should ponder more deeply now to make interpretive use of statistical series. All these types of research can be given added meaning by cross cultural comparisons.

More explicit methods and hypotheses will in themselves provide incentives for historical progress. They are primarily devices for stimulating insight and imagination, for shaking the mind loose from the tyranny of conventional words, unexamined clichés, and pleasantly familiar paths of thought.

Index

Format by Lydia Link
Set in Linotype Baskerville
Composed by Jackson Typesetting Company
Printed by Murray Printing Company
Bound by The Colonial Press
HARPER & ROW, PUBLISHERS, INCORPORATED

hARpER ✦ ᴛoRchbooKs

HUMANITIES AND SOCIAL SCIENCES

American Studies

JOHN R. ALDEN: The American Revolution, 1775-1783.† Illus.   TB/3011

RAY STANNARD BAKER: Following the Color Line: American Negro Citizenship in the Progressive Era.‡ Illus. Edited by Dewey W. Grantham, Jr.   TB/3053

RAY A. BILLINGTON: The Far Western Frontier, 1830-1860.† Illus.   TB/3012

JOSEPH L. BLAU, Ed.: Cornerstones of Religious Freedom in America. Selected Basic Documents, Court Decisions and Public Statements. Enlarged and revised edition with new Intro. by Editor   TB/118

RANDOLPH S. BOURNE: War and the Intellectuals: Collected Essays, 1915-1919.‡ Edited by Carl Resek   TB/3043

A. RUSSELL BUCHANAN: The United States and World War II. † Illus.   Volume I TB/3044
                                          Volume II TB/3045

ABRAHAM CAHAN: The Rise of David Levinsky: a novel. Introduction by John Higham   TB/1028

JOSEPH CHARLES: The Origins of the American Party System   TB/1049

THOMAS C. COCHRAN: The Inner Revolution: Essays on the Social Sciences in History
                                                   TB/1140

T. C. COCHRAN & WILLIAM MILLER: The Age of Enterprise: A Social History of Industrial America
                                                   TB/1054

EDWARD S. CORWIN: American Constitutional History: Essays edited by Alpheus T. Mason and Gerald Garvey   TB/1136

FOSTER RHEA DULLES: America's Rise to World Power, 1898-1954.† Illus.   TB/3021

W. A. DUNNING: Reconstruction, Political and Economic, 1865-1877   TB/1073

A. HUNTER DUPREE: Science in the Federal Government: A History of Policies and Activities to 1940
                                                   TB/573

CLEMENT EATON: The Growth of Southern Civilization, 1790-1860.† Illus.   TB/3040

HAROLD U. FAULKNER: Politics, Reform and Expansion, 1890-1900.† Illus.   TB/3020

LOUIS FILLER: The Crusade against Slavery, 1830-1860.† Illus.   TB/3029

EDITORS OF FORTUNE: America in the Sixties: the Economy and the Society. Two-color charts TB/1015

LAWRENCE HENRY GIPSON: The Coming of the Revolution, 1763-1775.† Illus.   TB/3007

FRANCIS J. GRUND: Aristocracy in America: Jacksonian Democracy   TB/1001

ALEXANDER HAMILTON: The Reports of Alexander Hamilton.‡ Edited by Jacob E. Cooke   TB/3060

OSCAR HANDLIN, Editor: This Was America: As Recorded by European Travelers to the Western Shore in the Eighteenth, Nineteenth, and Twentieth Centuries. Illus.   TB/1119

MARCUS LEE HANSEN: The Atlantic Migration: 1607-1860. Edited by Arthur M. Schlesinger; Introduction by Oscar Handlin   TB/1052

MARCUS LEE HANSEN: The Immigrant in American History. Edited with a Foreword by Arthur Schlesinger, Sr.   TB/1120

JOHN D. HICKS: Republican Ascendancy, 1921-1933.† Illus.   TB/3041

JOHN HIGHAM, Ed.: The Reconstruction of American History   TB/1068

DANIEL R. HUNDLEY: Social Relations in our Southern States.‡ Edited by William R. Taylor TB/3058

ROBERT H. JACKSON: The Supreme Court in the American System of Government   TB/1106

THOMAS JEFFERSON: Notes on the State of Virginia.‡ Edited by Thomas Perkins Abernethy TB/3052

WILLIAM L. LANGER & S. EVERETT GLEASON: The Challenge to Isolation: The World Crisis of 1937-1940 and American Foreign Policy   Volume I TB/3054
                                          Volume II TB/3055

WILLIAM E. LEUCHTENBURG: Franklin D. Roosevelt and the New Deal, 1932-1940.† Illus.   TB/3025

LEONARD W. LEVY: Freedom of Speech and Press in Early American History: Legacy of Suppression
                                                   TB/1109

ARTHUR S. LINK: Woodrow Wilson and the Progressive Era, 1910-1917.† Illus.   TB/3023

ROBERT GREEN McCLOSKEY: American Conservatism in the Age of Enterprise, 1865-1910 TB/1137

BERNARD MAYO: Myths and Men: Patrick Henry, George Washington, Thomas Jefferson TB/1108

JOHN C. MILLER: Alexander Hamilton and the Growth of the New Nation   TB/3057

JOHN C. MILLER: The Federalist Era, 1789-1801.† Illus.   TB/3027

---

† The New American Nation Series, edited by Henry Steele Commager and Richard B. Morris.

‡ American Perspectives series, edited by Bernard Wishy and William E. Leuchtenburg.

* The Rise of Modern Europe series, edited by William L. Langer.

❚ Researches in the Social, Cultural, and Behavioral Sciences, edited by Benjamin Nelson.

§ The Library of Religion and Culture, edited by Benjamin Nelson.

Σ Harper Modern Science Series, edited by James R. Newman.

ᵒ Not for sale in Canada.

PERRY MILLER: Errand into the Wilderness   TB/1139
PERRY MILLER & T. H. JOHNSON, Editors: The Puritans: *A Sourcebook of Their Writings*
Volume I   TB/1093
Volume II   TB/1094
GEORGE E. MOWRY: The Era of Theodore Roosevelt and the Birth of Modern America, 1900-1912.† *Illus.*
TB/3022
WALLACE NOTESTEIN: The English People on the Eve of Colonization, 1603-1630.† *Illus.*   TB/3006
RUSSEL BLAINE NYE: The Cultural Life of the New Nation, 1776-1801.† *Illus.*   TB/3026
RALPH BARTON PERRY: Puritanism and Democracy
TB/1138
GEORGE E. PROBST, Ed.: The Happy Republic: *A Reader in Tocqueville's America*   TB/1060
WALTER RAUSCHENBUSCH: Christianity and the Social Crisis.‡ *Edited by Robert D. Cross*   TB/3059
FRANK THISTLETHWAITE: America and the Atlantic Community: *Anglo-American Aspects, 1790-1850*
TB/1107
TWELVE SOUTHERNERS: I'll Take My Stand: *The South and the Agrarian Tradition. Introduction by Louis D. Rubin, Jr.; Biographical Essays by Virginia Rock*   TB/1072
A. F. TYLER: Freedom's Ferment: *Phases of American Social History from the Revolution to the Outbreak of the Civil War. Illus.*   TB/1074
GLYNDON G. VAN DEUSEN: The Jacksonian Era, 1828-1848.† *Illus.*   TB/3028
WALTER E. WEYL: The New Democracy: *An Essay on Certain Political and Economic Tendencies in the United States.‡ Edited by Charles Forcey*   TB/3042
LOUIS B. WRIGHT: The Cultural Life of the American Colonies, 1607-1763.† *Illus.*   TB/3005
LOUIS B. WRIGHT: Culture on the Moving Frontier
TB/1053

Anthropology & Sociology

BERNARD BERELSON, Ed.: The Behavioral Sciences Today   TB/1127
JOSEPH B. CASAGRANDE, Ed.: In the Company of Man: *20 Portraits of Anthropological Informants. Illus.*   TB/3047
W. E. LE GROS CLARK: The Antecedents of Man: *An Introduction to the Evolution of the Primates.° Illus.*
TB/559
THOMAS C. COCHRAN: The Inner Revolution: *Essays on the Social Sciences in History*
TB/1140
ALLISON DAVIS & JOHN DOLLARD: Children of Bondage: *The Personality Development of Negro Youth in the Urban South*▮   TB/3049
ST. CLAIR DRAKE & HORACE R. CAYTON: Black Metropolis: *A Study of Negro Life in a Northern City. Introduction by Everett C. Hughes. Tables, maps, charts and graphs*   Volume I   TB/1086
Volume II   TB/1087
CORA DU BOIS: The People of Alor. *New Preface by the author. Illus.*   Volume I   TB/1042
Volume II   TB/1043
LEON FESTINGER, HENRY W. RIECKEN & STANLEY SCHACHTER: When Prophecy Fails: *A Social and Psychological Account of a Modern Group that Predicted the Destruction of the World*▮   TB/1132
RAYMOND FIRTH, Ed.: Man and Culture: *An Evaluation of the Work of Bronislaw Malinowski*▮°
TB/1133

L. S. B. LEAKEY: Adam's Ancestors: *The Evolution of Man and his Culture. Illus.*   TB/1019
KURT LEWIN: Field Theory in Social Science: *Selected Theoretical Papers.*▮ *Edited with a Foreword by Dorwin Cartwright*   TB/1135
ROBERT H. LOWIE: Primitive Society. *Introduction by Fred Eggan*   TB/1056
BENJAMIN NELSON: Religious Traditions and the Spirit of Capitalism: *From the Church Fathers to Jeremy Bentham*   TB/1130
TALCOTT PARSONS & EDWARD A. SHILS, Editors: Toward a General Theory of Action: *Theoretical Foundations for the Social Sciences*   TB/1083
JOHN H. ROHRER & MUNRO S. EDMONSON, Eds.: The Eighth Generation Grows Up: *Cultures and Personalities of New Orleans Negroes*▮   TB/3050
ARNOLD ROSE: The Negro in America: *The Condensed Version of Gunnar Myrdal's An American Dilemma. New Introduction by the Author; Foreword by Gunnar Myrdal*   TB/3048
KURT SAMUELSSON: Religion and Economic Action: *A Critique of Max Weber's The Protestant Ethic and the Spirit of Capitalism.*▮° *Trans. by E. G. French; Ed. with Intro. by D. C. Coleman*   TB/1131
PITIRIM SOROKIN: Contemporary Sociological Theories: *Through the First Quarter of the Twentieth Century*   TB/3046
MAURICE R. STEIN: The Eclipse of Community: *An Interpretation of American Studies. New Introduction by the Author*   TB/1128
SIR EDWARD TYLOR: The Origins of Culture. *Part I of "Primitive Culture."§ Introduction by Paul Radin*
TB/33
SIR EDWARD TYLOR: Religion in Primitive Culture. *Part II of "Primitive Culture."§ Introduction by Paul Radin*   TB/34
W. LLOYD WARNER & Associates: Democracy in Jonesville: *A Study in Quality and Inequality***
TB/1129
W. LLOYD WARNER: A Black Civilization: *A Study of an Australian Tribe.*▮ *Illus.*   TB/3056
W. LLOYD WARNER: Social Class in America: *The Evaluation of Status*   TB/1013

Art and Art History

EMILE MÂLE: The Gothic Image: *Religious Art in France of the Thirteenth Century.§ 190 illus.*   TB/44
MILLARD MEISS: Painting in Florence and Siena after the Black Death. *169 illus.*   TB/1148
ERWIN PANOFSKY: Studies in Iconology: *Humanistic Themes in the Art of the Renaissance. 180 illustrations*   TB/1077
ALEXANDRE PIANKOFF: The Shrines of Tut-Ankh-Amon. *Edited by N. Rambova. 117 illus.*   TB/2011
JEAN SEZNEC: The Survival of the Pagan Gods: *The Mythological Tradition and Its Place in Renaissance Humanism and Art. 108 illustrations*   TB/2004
OTTO VON SIMSON: The Gothic Cathedral: *Origins of Gothic Architecture and the Medieval Concept of Order. 58 illus.*   TB/2018
HEINRICH ZIMMER: Myths and Symbols in Indian Art and Civilization. *70 illustrations*   TB/2005

Business, Economics & Economic History

REINHARD BENDIX: Work and Authority in Industry: *Ideologies of Management in the Course of Industrialization*   TB/3035

2

4

ST.-JOHN PERSE: Seamarks   TB/2002
O. E. RÖLVAAG: Giants in the Earth. *Introduction by Einar Haugen*   TB/3504
GEORGE SANTAYANA: Interpretations of Poetry and Religion§   TB/9
C. P. SNOW: Time of Hope: *a novel*   TB/1040
DOROTHY VAN GHENT: The English Novel: *Form and Function*   TB/1050
E. B. WHITE: One Man's Meat. *Introduction by Walter Blair*   TB/3505
MORTON DAUWEN ZABEL, Editor: Literary Opinion in America   Volume I TB/3013
                                      Volume II TB/3014

Myth, Symbol & Folklore

JOSEPH CAMPBELL, Editor: Pagan and Christian Mysteries. *Illus.*   TB/2013
MIRCEA ELIADE: Cosmos and History: *The Myth of the Eternal Return*§   TB/2050
C. G. JUNG & C. KERÉNYI: Essays on a Science of Mythology: *The Myths of the Divine Child and the Divine Maiden*   TB/2014
ERWIN PANOFSKY: Studies in Iconology: *Humanistic Themes in the Art of the Renaissance. 180 illustrations*   TB/1077
JEAN SEZNEC: The Survival of the Pagan Gods: *The Mythological Tradition and its Place in Renaissance Humanism and Art. 108 illustrations*   TB/2004
HELLMUT WILHELM: Change: *Eight Lectures on the I Ching*   TB/2019
HEINRICH ZIMMER: Myths and Symbols in Indian Art and Civilization. *70 illustrations*   TB/2005

Philosophy

HENRI BERGSON: Time and Free Will: *An Essay on the Immediate Data of Consciousness*° TB/1021
H. J. BLACKHAM: Six Existentialist Thinkers: *Kierkegaard, Nietzsche, Jaspers, Marcel, Heidegger, Sartre*°   TB/1002
ERNST CASSIRER: Rousseau, Kant and Goethe. *Introduction by Peter Gay*   TB/1092
FREDERICK COPLESTON: Medieval Philosophy°
                                            TB/76
F. M. CORNFORD: From Religion to Philosophy: *A Study in the Origins of Western Speculation*§ TB/20
WILFRID DESAN: The Tragic Finale: *An Essay on the Philosophy of Jean-Paul Sartre*   TB/1030
PAUL FRIEDLÄNDER: Plato: *An Introduction*
                                            TB/2017
ETIENNE GILSON: Dante and Philosophy   TB/1089
WILLIAM CHASE GREENE: Moira: *Fate, Good, and Evil in Greek Thought*   TB/1104
W. K. C. GUTHRIE: The Greek Philosophers: *From Thales to Aristotle*°   TB/1008
F. H. HEINEMANN: Existentialism and the Modern Predicament   TB/28
IMMANUEL KANT: The Doctrine of Virtue, *being Part II of The Metaphysic of Morals. Translated with Notes and Introduction by Mary J. Gregor. Foreword by H. J. Paton*   TB/110
IMMANUEL KANT: Lectures on Ethics.§ *Introduction by Lewis W. Beck*   TB/105
WILLARD VAN ORMAN QUINE: From a Logical Point of View: *Logico-Philosophical Essays*   TB/566

BERTRAND RUSSELL et al.: The Philosophy of Bertrand Russell. *Edited by Paul Arthur Schilpp*
                                      Volume I TB/1095
                                      Volume II TB/1096
L. S. STEBBING: A Modern Introduction to Logic
                                            TB/538
ALFRED NORTH WHITEHEAD: Process and Reality: *An Essay in Cosmology*   TB/1033
WILHELM WINDELBAND: A History of Philosophy I: *Greek, Roman, Medieval*   TB/38
WILHELM WINDELBAND: A History of Philosophy II: *Renaissance, Enlightenment, Modern*   TB/39

Philosophy of History

NICOLAS BERDYAEV: The Beginning and the End§
                                            TB/14
NICOLAS BERDYAEV: The Destiny of Man   TB/61
WILHELM DILTHEY: Pattern and Meaning in History: *Thoughts on History and Society.*° *Edited with an Introduction by H. P. Rickman*   TB/1075
RAYMOND KLIBANSKY & H. J. PATON, Eds.: Philosophy and History: *The Ernst Cassirer Festschrift. Illus.*   TB/1115
JOSE ORTEGA Y GASSET: The Modern Theme. *Introduction by Jose Ferrater Mora*   TB/1038
KARL R. POPPER: The Poverty of Historicism°
                                            TB/1126
W. H. WALSH: Philosophy of History: *An Introduction*   TB/1020

Political Science & Government

JEREMY BENTHAM: The Handbook of Political Fallacies: *Introduction by Crane Brinton*   TB/1069
KENNETH E. BOULDING: Conflict and Defense: *A General Theory*   TB/3024
CRANE BRINTON: English Political Thought in the Nineteenth Century   TB/1071
EDWARD S. CORWIN: American Constitutional History: *Essays edited by Alpheus T. Mason and Gerald Garvey*   TB/1136
ROBERT DAHL & CHARLES E. LINDBLOM: Politics, Economics, and Welfare: *Planning and Politico-Economic Systems Resolved into Basic Social Processes*   TB/3037
JOHN NEVILLE FIGGIS: Political Thought from Gerson to Grotius: 1414-1625: *Seven Studies. Introduction by Garrett Mattingly*   TB/1032
F. L. GANSHOF: Feudalism   TB/1058
G. P. GOOCH: English Democratic Ideas in the Seventeenth Century   TB/1006
ROBERT H. JACKSON: The Supreme Court in the American System of Government   TB/1106
DAN N. JACOBS, Ed.: The New Communist Manifesto and Related Documents   TB/1078
DAN N. JACOBS & HANS BAERWALD, Eds.: Chinese Communism: *Selected Documents*   TB/3031
ROBERT GREEN McCLOSKEY: American Conservatism in the Age of Enterprise, 1865-1910   TB/1137
KINGSLEY MARTIN: French Liberal Thought in the Eighteenth Century: *A Study of Political Ideas from Bayle to Condorcet*   TB/1114
JOHN STUART MILL: On Bentham and Coleridge. *Introduction by F. R. Leavis*   TB/1070
JOHN B. MORRALL: Political Thought in Medieval Times   TB/1076

5

KARL R. POPPER: The Open Society and Its Enemies
Volume I: *The Spell of Plato* TB/1101
Volume II: *The High Tide of Prophecy: Hegel, Marx, and the Aftermath* TB/1102
JOSEPH A. SCHUMPETER: Capitalism, Socialism and Democracy TB/3008

Psychology

ALFRED ADLER: Problems of Neurosis. *Introduction by Heinz L. Ansbacher* TB/1145
ANTON T. BOISEN: The Exploration of the Inner World: *A Study of Mental Disorder and Religious Experience* TB/87
LEON FESTINGER, HENRY W. RIECKEN, STANLEY SCHACHTER: When Prophecy Fails: *A Social and Psychological Study of a Modern Group that Predicted the Destruction of the World* ‖ TB/1132
SIGMUND FREUD: On Creativity and the Unconscious: *Papers on the Psychology of Art, Literature, Love, Religion.*§ *Intro. by Benjamin Nelson* TB/45
C. JUDSON HERRICK: The Evolution of Human Nature TB/545
ALDOUS HUXLEY: The Devils of Loudun: *A Study in the Psychology of Power Politics and Mystical Religion in the France of Cardinal Richelieu*§° TB/60
WILLIAM JAMES: Psychology: *The Briefer Course. Edited with an Intro. by Gordon Allport* TB/1034
C. G. JUNG: Psychological Reflections. *Edited by Jolande Jacobi* TB/2001
C. G. JUNG: Symbols of Transformation: *An Analysis of the Prelude to a Case of Schizophrenia. Illus.*
Volume I TB/2009
Volume II TB/2010
C. G. JUNG & C. KERÉNYI: Essays on a Science of Mythology: *The Myths of the Divine Child and the Divine Maiden* TB/2014
SOREN KIERKEGAARD: Repetition: *An Essay in Experimental Psychology. Translated with Introduction & Notes by Walter Lowrie* TB/117
KARL MENNINGER: Theory of Psychoanalytic Technique TB/1144
ERICH NEUMANN: Amor and Psyche: *The Psychic Development of the Feminine* TB/2012
ERICH NEUMANN: The Origins and History of Consciousness Volume I *Illus.* TB/2007
Volume II TB/2008
C. P. OBERNDORF: A History of Psychoanalysis in America TB/1147
JEAN PIAGET, BÄRBEL INHELDER, & ALINA SZEMINSKA: The Child's Conception of Geometry TB/1146

RELIGION

Ancient & Classical

J. H. BREASTED: Development of Religion and Thought in Ancient Egypt. *Introduction by John A. Wilson* TB/57
HENRI FRANKFORT: Ancient Egyptian Religion: *An Interpretation* TB/77
WILLIAM CHASE GREENE: Moira: *Fate, Good and Evil in Greek Thought* TB/1104

G. RACHEL LEVY: Religious Conceptions of the Stone Age *and their Influence upon European Thought. Illus. Introduction by Henri Frankfort* TB/106
MARTIN P. NILSSON: Greek Folk Religion. *Foreword by Arthur Darby Nock* TB/78
ALEXANDRE PIANKOFF: The Shrines of Tut-Ankh-Amon. *Edited by N. Rambova. 117 illus.* TB/2011
H. J. ROSE: Religion in Greece and Rome TB/55

Biblical Thought & Literature

W. F. ALBRIGHT: The Biblical Period from Abraham to Ezra TB/102
C. K. BARRETT, Ed.: The New Testament Background: *Selected Documents* TB/86
C. H. DODD: The Authority of the Bible TB/43
M. S. ENSLIN: Christian Beginnings TB/5
M. S. ENSLIN: The Literature of the Christian Movement TB/6
H. E. FOSDICK: A Guide to Understanding the Bible TB/2
H. H. ROWLEY: The Growth of the Old Testament TB/107
D. WINTON THOMAS, Ed.: Documents from Old Testament Times TB/85

Christianity: Origins & Early Development

ADOLF DEISSMANN: Paul: *A Study in Social and Religious History* TB/15
EDWARD GIBBON: The Triumph of Christendom in the Roman Empire (*Chaps. XV-XX of "Decline and Fall," J. B. Bury edition*).§ *Illus.* TB/46
MAURICE GOGUEL: Jesus and the Origins of Christianity.° *Introduction by C. Leslie Mitton*
Volume I: *Prolegomena to the Life of Jesus* TB/65
Volume II: *The Life of Jesus* TB/66
EDGAR J. GOODSPEED: A Life of Jesus TB/1
ADOLF HARNACK: The Mission and Expansion of Christianity *in the First Three Centuries. Introduction by Jaroslav Pelikan* TB/92
R. K. HARRISON: The Dead Sea Scrolls: *An Introduction*° TB/84
EDWIN HATCH: The Influence of Greek Ideas on Christianity.§ *Introduction and Bibliography by Frederick C. Grant* TB /18
ARTHUR DARBY NOCK: Early Gentile Christianity and Its Hellenistic Background TB/111
ARTHUR DARBY NOCK: St. Paul° TB/104
JOHANNES WEISS: Earliest Christianity: *A History of the Period A.D. 30-150. Introduction and Bibliography by Frederick C. Grant* Volume I TB/53
Volume II TB/54

Christianity: The Middle Ages, The Reformation, and After

G. P. FEDOTOV: The Russian Religious Mind: *Kievan Christianity, the tenth to the thirteenth centuries* TB/70
ÉTIENNE GILSON: Dante and Philosophy TB/1089
WILLIAM HALLER: The Rise of Puritanism TB/22
JOHAN HUIZINGA: Erasmus and the Age of Reformation. *Illus.* TB/19

8

Philosophy of Science

R. B. BRAITHWAITE: Scientific Explanation   TB/515

J. BRONOWSKI: Science and Human Values. *Illus.*
TB/505

ALBERT EINSTEIN: Philosopher-Scientist. *Edited by*
Paul A. Schilpp   Volume I   TB/502
Volume II   TB/503

WERNER HEISENBERG: Physics and Philosophy: *The*
Revolution in Modern Science. Introduction by F. S.
C. Northrop   TB/549

JOHN MAYNARD KEYNES: A Treatise on Probability.° *Introduction by N. R. Hanson*   TB/557

STEPHEN TOULMIN: Foresight and Understanding:
An Enquiry into the Aims of Science. Foreword by
Jacques Barzun   TB/564

STEPHEN TOULMIN: The Philosophy of Science: *An*
Introduction   TB/513

G. J. WHITROW: The Natural Philosophy of Time°
TB/563

Physics and Cosmology

DAVID BOHM: Causality and Chance in Modern
Physics. *Foreword by Louis de Broglie*   TB/536

P. W. BRIDGMAN: The Nature of Thermodynamics
TB/537

A. C. CROMBIE, Ed.: Turning Point in Physics   TB/535

C. V. DURELL: Readable Relativity. *Foreword by Free-*
man J. Dyson   TB/530

ARTHUR EDDINGTON: Space, Time and Gravitation:
An outline of the General Relativity Theory   TB/510

GEORGE GAMOW: Biography of Physics∑   TB/567

MAX JAMMER: Concepts of Force: *A Study in the*
Foundation of Dynamics   TB/550

MAX JAMMER: Concepts of Mass *in Classical and*
Modern Physics   TB/571

MAX JAMMER: Concepts of Space: *The History of*
Theories of Space in Physics. Foreword by Albert
Einstein   TB/533

EDMUND WHITTAKER: History of the Theories of
Aether and Electricity
Volume I: *The Classical Theories*   TB/531
Volume II: *The Modern Theories*   TB/532

G. J. WHITROW: The Structure and Evolution of the
Universe: *An Introduction to Cosmology. Illus.*
TB/504

A LETTER TO THE READER

Overseas, there is considerable belief that we are a country of extreme conservatism and that we cannot accommodate to social change.

Books about America in the hands of readers abroad can help change those ideas.

The U. S. Information Agency cannot, by itself, meet the vast need for books about the United States.

You can help.

Harper Torchbooks provides three packets of books on American history, economics, sociology, literature and politics to help meet the need.

To send a packet of Torchbooks [*] overseas, all you need do is send your check for $7 (which includes cost of shipping) to Harper & Row. The U. S. Information Agency will distribute the books to libraries, schools, and other centers all over the world.

I ask every American to support this program, part of a worldwide BOOKS USA campaign.

I ask you to share in the opportunity to help tell others about America.

EDWARD R. MURROW
Director,
U. S. Information Agency

[*retailing at $10.85 to $12.00]

PACKET I: Twentieth Century America

Dulles/America's Rise to World Power, 1898-1954
Cochran/The American Business System, 1900-1955
Zabel, Editor/Literary Opinion in America (two volumes)
Drucker/The New Society: *The Anatomy of Industrial Order*
Fortune Editors/America in the Sixties: *The Economy and the Society*

PACKET II: American History

Billington/The Far Western Frontier, 1830-1860
Mowry/The Era of Theodore Roosevelt and the
    Birth of Modern America, 1900-1912
Faulkner/Politics, Reform, and Expansion, 1890-1900
Cochran & Miller/The Age of Enterprise: *A Social History of
    Industrial America*
Tyler/Freedom's Ferment: *American Social History from the
    Revolution to the Civil War*

PACKET III: American History

Hansen/The Atlantic Migration, 1607-1860
Degler/Out of Our Past: *The Forces that Shaped Modern America*
Probst, Editor/The Happy Republic: *A Reader in Tocqueville's America*
Alden/The American Revolution, 1775-1783
Wright/The Cultural Life of the American Colonies, 1607-1763

*Your gift will be acknowledged directly to you by the overseas recipient.
Simply fill out the coupon, detach and mail with your check or money order.*

HARPER & ROW, PUBLISHERS · BOOKS USA DEPT.
49 East 33rd Street, New York 16, N. Y.

Packet I ☐   Packet II ☐   Packet III ☐

Please send the BOOKS USA library packet(s) indicated above, in my
name, to the area checked below. Enclosed is my remittance in the
amount of _____ for _____ packet(s) at $7.00 each.

_____ Africa   _____ Latin America

_____ Far East   _____ Near East

Name_____

Address_____

_____

NOTE: This offer expires December 31, 1966.